William Marchant, André Chevrillon

Romantic India

William Marchant, André Chevrillon

Romantic India

ISBN/EAN: 9783744694407

Printed in Europe, USA, Canada, Australia, Japan

Cover: Foto ©Andreas Hilbeck / pixelio.de

More available books at **www.hansebooks.com**

ROMANTIC INDIA

Translated from the French of

ANDRÉ CHEVRILLON

BY

WILLIAM MARCHANT

London
WILLIAM HEINEMANN
MDCCCXCVII

CONTENTS

CHAP.		PAGE
I.	AT SEA	1
II.	CEYLON. BUDDHISM	11
III.	PONDICHÉRY. CALCUTTA	44
IV.	THE HIMALAYA. DARJILING	56
V.	BENARES. BRAHMANISM. HINDUISM	74
VI.	LUCKNOW. CAWNPUR. AGRA	158
VII.	DELHI. JAIPUR	190
VIII.	BOMBAY	219
IX.	ELURA	233
X.	THE VOYAGE	248

ROMANTIC INDIA

CHAPTER I

AT SEA

OFF MASSOUAH, *November* 3.

FOR three days we have been going straight toward the South, and, the other morning, just as the faint outline of Sinai was vanishing upon the horizon, we came into the regions of excessive heat. It is a moist, close heat, in which the muscles are relaxed, the whole body seems melting and sinking away—a heat oppressive, prostrating by night as well as day. At times one's clothing seems to burn the skin and to become unendurable. There is no going below for meals : all day long we lie inert in our deck-chairs. A double tent shuts us in, completely hiding both sea and sky; and still the eyes become inflamed with the excess of light.

Coleridge's weird poem of the "Ancient Mariner" comes to my mind. Thus he sailed, oppressed with a strange numbness, a kind of torpor, that cannot be shaken off. There is not the slightest breeze; our speed outruns the light wind which follows in our wake; the fiery air is heavy and motionless; we are not conscious of the ship's advance. There is something unnatural about a sea like this; it seems under a spell, struck by a malediction; it has not the fluidity of water. Sometimes a glimpse of it can be seen through a rent in the canvas shelter, and it is a sheet of molten glass, inert, dense, heavy; nothing could be more dismal than its monotonous glare in the sunlight. At a distance it steams, and this whitish, quivering haze, this tremulous fog, shuts us in, hiding the sea a few miles away. Beyond, the imagination depicts fiery wildernesses, terrific solitudes void of all life.

By night the sensation of rapid motion, of slipping away into some unknown world, recurs. The constellations are seen to be leaving their familiar places. In each twenty-four hours they have gone so many degrees farther northward. The Great Bear is plunging downward to the horizon: now he has lost two, now three, of his big stars: now he is gone completely; and in front of us rise, sparkling, the four points of the Southern Cross, while slowly the great belt of the Milky Way is pushed back.

Lying upon the deck, which by night is deserted, one hears the incessant rustling of the water; looking fixedly at the stars, you feel conscious of an ascent toward the equator, of a going up over the convexity of the globe, over this great dark ball that hangs in space; and at certain moments you seem to see the measured movement of the heavenly bodies—those eternal beacons, millions of leagues away, in inconceivable depths of space.

One o'clock A.M.—The mercury stands at 100°, and still it is a moist heat. One falls into a strange drowsiness interrupted by feverish awakenings, when the swarms of stars that suddenly appear frighten one. Then follows heavy sleep, a sinking away into black darkness, wherein the brain gropes confusedly, amid flashes of sharp pain and sudden swoons, dropping abruptly off into unconsciousness, or, again, feebly striving against the crushing torpor. After this, a sort of fevered excitement, a singular lucidity of mind, crowds of recollections, whole periods of life appearing entire; and, of a sudden, around you, the wondrous tropical night, large and luminous, deep blue between the stars which, low on the horizon, blaze as bright as those in the zenith. Nor is the sea dark now, but full of a deep light, illumined in its depths by all the absorbed sunshine of the day, and on its surface by countless splashes of starlight.

Four o'clock.—The white stellar dust overhead is gone. Only the great stars still throb with a pale light, and a faint rose colour flushes in the east, so faint one can but just see it. Suddenly it has gone all round the edge of the sky, like some pervasive fluid of infinite tenuity, melting by exquisite gradations into the pallid spaces overhead. The blue of the sea becomes visible, a chaste, dull, neutral blue, not yet touched by the sun. The horizon retreats, becomes defined, and the watery space broadens in the daylight.

November 5.

We reached Aden last night. Awaking, in the morning, the coast is visible. How describe it? It is a negro land, nude and black, under a blazing sun—a huge bank of coal, rising out of the sea; no vapour, no vegetation softens the sharp silhouette of the gloomy volcanic rocks outlined with implacable hardness against the blue of the sky. Contrasted with this landscape of Erebus, the sea again seems liquid, cool, of a delicate greenish tint. On the left lies the Arab coast, a dazzling white wilderness, melting in the distance into white undulations of the heated atmosphere.

We shall be off again almost immediately, and have no time to go on shore. Looking from the deck, I see upon a road groups of superb negroes draped in red—a red victorious and brutal in the sunlight, flaming against the blackness of the landscape; meagre, withered camels, moving their slender, thick-lipped heads from side to side with gentle, haughty undulation; files of little Scriptural asses; lastly, two English soldiers with tennis rackets. They are all coming down toward the shore on a road of cinders along below the carbonised rocks.

On our deck some oily Jews, with greedy, piteous faces, weep, endeavouring to persuade us to buy ostrich feathers. Invincibly persistent, they cling to us, they surround us with their timid yet eager gestures. What a contrast between their lamentable aspect, as of whipped dogs, and the gaiety of these supple negro boys with their broad, white laugh! The well-developed, active bodies are lustrous in the sunlight. A very small black boy, scarcely a five-year-old baby, with irresistible grimaces, with the graceful clumsiness of a young kitten, is determined, at all hazards, to sell me an old East India Company rupee. He forces it into my hand, and the touch of the little paw, dry and parchment-like, reminds me of a monkey's.

We throw small coins into the water, and the whole little crowd dive for them. They jump off like frogs, their heads cleaving the lustrous surface of the water, and the eye follows the black kicking until it disappears in the green depths. Other boys paddle around the ship, astride upon tree-trunks, urging themselves on with a smacking of the lips and with strident cries like the chirping of crickets. They are the offspring of the sea, rejoicing in life and movement, like insects hatched in the sand and hopping about upon the shore. Now and then a shark snaps one up, but what does it matter? What matter if a swallow darts upon a fly? One of these children has had an arm taken off by a snap of the powerful jaws; you find yourself wondering that the arm has not grown again, like a lobster's claw.

Four English ships, arriving last night, have sailed again immediately; and our steamer, long, slender, lying low on the water, its two raking funnels smoking all the time, seems like a runner detained against his will, eager to get away, impatient to resume his race and arrive on the farther coast of Japan!

At nine o'clock I hear begin that motion of the screw which is now to last uninterruptedly for a week.

November 6.

Under the double tent the evenings are disagreeable, with stale odours of tobacco, of cooking, of oil from the engine-room. It has become tiresome to pace the deck with one's fellow-passengers, exchanging commonplaces on European politics—this is to endure all the boredom of civilised life. One would gladly escape being elbowed by this crowd moving about under the electric light, like any crowd in Hyde Park or the Champs-Elysées; tall, correct Englishmen, mindful of their digestion, and at this hour making the fifth mile of their constitutional; French functionaries who smoke, leaning against the quarter-nettings; yawning loungers extended in deck-chairs; bare-legged children who drive hoops, while their mammas embroider or read the latest novel. From the ladies' cabin come waltz-tunes, as of hand-organs in London or Paris streets: "The Beautiful Blue Danube," or "Sweet Dream Faces," or that eternal "Kathleen Mavourneen," which, with all its foolish sentimentality of words, has the irresistible charm of an old French chanson—how hackneyed it all is! And yet how hard it is to put all these commonplace things completely out of the mind! In truth, it requires a great effort of the imagination to grasp the strange reality: to be conscious of the black expanse upon which we lie, itself moving in the darkness outside of all these human noises; the ten thousand feet straight down between us and the submarine ground weighed upon by this black watery mass—these unknown depths where things have remained changeless through eons.

But go quite aft, and put your head out from under the tent: the people who are walking the deck disappear, the waltzes cease, the Edison light goes out. A strong wind smites you in the face, taking you by surprise. At first you see nothing but the empty blackness of space; suddenly the tall masts with the crossed yards lift their immense geometric lines, swaying slowly against the bright stars and the swarming cosmic dust; a pervasive low noise fills the darkness. At your feet, under a black whirl, phosphorescent masses, bluish globes, fly, and, beaten madly by the screw, make a broad milky path—a great undefined furrow in the darkness. And you feel yourself alone upon the huge thing which is running blindly on, lost in the night, between the mystery of the sea, brooding a luminous life, and the mystery of the sky, where shine, in whitish patches, suns as yet unformed—between these two overwhelming blacknesses in which float, coming one knows not whence, the beginnings of worlds, and the beginnings of life.

November 7.

In the morning, but few passengers on deck. All day long the ship rolls heavily: she lies down slowly to starboard, recovers, lies down to port, and her three masts describe their regular oscillation against the sky. The huge creature, whose dull heart-throbs one feels, quivers all over, exults in this slow, mighty movement, in this profound rhythmic oscillation, in this going forward through the heavy blue seas which lift the surface in vast glassy domes, in all this disturbance which comes to us from the South, from the great watery spaces which cover the austral hemisphere. Separated from us only by the bulwarks there is a liquid tumult, a merry uproar of glittering foam falling back into the blue, there is a white water-dust spread in sheets, dazzling with light, and running off in sinuous furrows with a great noise as of tearing silk.

Beyond is the immense disk of the sea, of a marvellous blue, and on the starboard side burning like molten metal; the barren sea, burning under the fury of the blazing sun—the lord who from on high devours the heavens and fills all space with his shining; only an infinite, gloomy splendour, only these brute forces of heat and light, only these eternal things whose indifference crushes us—and no life at all, for the little flying-fish, springing back and forth over the angry surface, seem but flames thrown out from it like arrows of white fire.

After a time this great blaze of light makes one sad, and weighs down the heart with an extreme depression. It is easy to understand the homesickness of men of the North condemned to sail these Southern seas. Here the infinite has no vague gentleness, no melancholy charm, alluring and tempting, no subtle sadness whose very pang is a pleasure. It crushes and stupefies, and the whole being sinks under it, incapable of any effort to rally.

As one thus lies inert, a whole inner world of memories awakens; it grows, and fills the mind. It is an enfeebling besetment, but one has not strength to fight it off; it is a half-dream, very simple, yet weighted heavily with emotion. A scene appears as through a mist torn apart, then closing in again : through heavy masses of foliage falls a greenish light, there is a muddy bit of road between patches of yellow broom; sad little trees writhe against a grey sky. There are cottage-roofs, lustrous, wet with rain. Why can I not to-day dispel this vision of a little place near the gloomy harbour of Brest ? Still I see it. The place is not far from Portsic. There is complete solitude ; bare fields, sad and wintry, divided into wan squares, and bounded by low, black hedges. The wind is coming up, and clouds come with it; they rise higher, and gradually weave a pallid veil over the sky. Three trees graze each other with their slender branches. Behind is the Goulet ; how cold and grey the water, fretted by a slight ripple which is touched at one point by a trembling ray of pallid sunlight ! This ripple frets the stream between banks the colour of rusted iron. On these banks not a detail, not an accident of colour, only the hard, rough outline. There is a profound sensation of melancholy, bitter, and not temporary but enduring. These rocks, this gorse, this stream, this little icy wind—all this has suffered thus for ever, rigorously and patiently. Long, long has this grey water shivered between its walls of rusty iron. Presently, something strange is noticeable ; upon this rough promontory of rock, high up against the pale sky, there is what seem like splashes and trails of blood ; there are reddish lights, mysterious gleams, motionless, dismal. Then one is aware that this also is water, but infinitely remote, as in another world. And beyond lies darkness, ashen, cold, dense—where a distant sea, crimsoned by an invisible sun, fades away, vanishes, ends—like suffering absorbed in nothingness.

CHAPTER II

CEYLON BUDDHISM

YESTERDAY, as we were playing quoits, a little English girl, pale and discontented-looking, promised the captain a smile, if we should reach Colombo this evening.

The captain will win his smile: at five o'clock foggy stains appear on the horizon; about six, under a lowering sky, heavy with great violet-coloured clouds, a grove of cocoanut-trees becomes visible. Drawing nearer, we are able to distinguish a host of tall, stiff, slender trunks, bursting, by an oblique impulse, into a foliage of palm-leaves above. It is a vast forest, which seems to rise out of the sea. Even within two miles of land it is impossible to see the ground: there is only the dense growth upon it,—in every direction, this mighty vegetation overflowing with strength and sap,—the great equatorial vegetation, which springs out of ground soaked with rains and spreads wide its enormous leaves in the furnace-heat of the air.

We have not yet reached the land, and still, the sensation of this equatorial world is already very distinct. There is not the limpid, liquid blue of the classic East. Here, both sea and sky are violent, surcharged, so to speak. You feel that this is a place of storms and typhoons, a region situated on the girdle of the globe, looking toward a hemisphere of ocean—an overwhelming nature, under the vertical sun.

Meantime the sea grows dark; there are flushes of red across it, and spaces of undulation. These disappear, and there remains only a dull purplish lustre, pulsating under the tumultuous sky. Overhead, a chaos of light and colours; in the west, a vague radiance of a soft rose-tint; in the east, enormous cloud-masses rolling up, piling themselves high, then breaking down into fantastic shapes, in violets, greens, and flaming orange. Then all becoming colourless, there remain only black heaps, masses of gigantic dead shapes.

But the heavy, oily water still gives out a mysterious light which projects itself into the wan space. On the surface, a swarm of black objects—crawling among the waves, in pirogues, upon gliding trunks of trees—gather around the ship's side with deafening outcries. Then, of a sudden, in two minutes' time, all this disappears into the night, an impenetrable, stifling night, later filled by a heavy, violent, warm rain.

Having landed, I can see nothing, so dense is the darkness. Farther on, by the gaslight, I conjecture broad, straight avenues, with red soil, bordered by great gardens and palm-groves. The heat, endurable upon the water, is overwhelming here. The air, motionless and laden with the disturbing perfume of invisible flowers, weighs upon the mute city. Figures in narrow white garments, moving very quickly, barefooted, silent, graze us in passing, and disappear. This is altogether a new world, very different from the East as we know it in Egypt. Yes, one is very far away from home in this silence, this darkness, these heavy perfumes, this moist heat.

The Oriental Hotel is a large and comfortable building. The proprietress, a most correct Englishwoman, installs me, giving brief orders that servants receive with silent inclinations of the head. I have a great whitewashed room, entirely without furniture, except a little iron bedstead covered with a mosquito netting, and a deep arm-chair of cool straw, in which I recline during the silent, oppressive hours; on the ceiling is an odd-looking spot —a little, motionless lizard; then two, three little lizards, watching me with very sharp eyes.

In the long corridors crowds of Bengalese and Cinhalese servants, slender and gentle-looking. They glide noiselessly, with timid gestures, very respectful in the presence of the tall, solid Europeans, the handsome, muscular Englishmen, who, in evening dress, with shining white shirt-fronts, and the air of superior and unapproachable beings, make their way into the great dining-room.

It is a very handsome dining-room, full of passing Europeans, black stains in the white Asiatic crowd. It is like a great restaurant, situated where the highways of the world cross. At these tables are travellers from the opposite sides of the globe; passengers on the *Paramatta*, which sails to-morrow for Australia and New Zealand; French army officers; passengers on the *Caledonian*, which goes on to-night to Singapore and Saigon; Chinese on their way to Europe; English civilians going out to administer India.

Opposite me at table four Frenchmen, rich *bourgeois*, who, having had enough of Scotland and Switzerland, are on the way to Japan : Parisians by birth and race, *flâneurs du boulevard*, readers of the *Figaro*, *habitués* of the Palais Royal, admirers of M. Sarcey, republicans and liberals after the school of M. Thiers; one a laureate of the *Académie des Sciences morales;* all four typical of French education, of the *Lycée* and *l'École de Droit*, and of the boulevard. Two of them are well versed in literature and philosophy — the philosophy of Victor Hugo and of M. Paul Bert. With this, a raciness somewhat cynical but brilliant,—a clear head, visibly bewildered, however, at sight of a world which seems to be able to do without Paris. A third is more simple, of a stronger and sturdier growth, more sanguine and rugged, more frankly cheerful, getting more pleasure out of life, noisy, and "a ladies' man"; not quite so much the epicure, a little more the glutton; precisely M. Zola's representative of the middle class, the plump *bourgeois* who, seated on his hearth-rug, digests his dinner. There they are, flushed, rapid in word and gesture. Mobile in face, in contrast with the blond, tranquil Englishmen and the graceful Cinhalese—two of them agreeably excited, the third man on his high horse, full-blown, expanded, his heart open; happier, more jovial, more simply egotistical than ever. He cries: "Bring us some good wine!" And the party drink champagne from goblets.

Two hundred guests are at dinner. The great punkahs swing slowly back and forth with regular and ample sweep, red, between high, whitewashed walls. Upon the lustrous tablecloths a profusion of blood-red flowers; and all around us in motion a multitude of Cinhalese servants, very serious, very gentle, a yellow shell comb at the top of the chignon, dark in their narrow white garments, mute, moving noiselessly on naked feet among the tables with their floral decorations and their crowd of guests.

November 10.

In the morning we walk about the city—a marvellous city, in which there is nothing to be seen but verdure, the plants hiding the houses. The atmosphere is damp and very hot, and penetrated through and through with moist light.

The streets are the avenues of a vast tropical garden. Palm-trees, ferns, ebony-trees, sandalwood, cinnamon-trees, camphor-trees, pineapples —plants with strong sap; the most prized hothouse flowers are at home here, growing without cultivation; and all this vegetable world gives out a strong, heavy perfume. You feel that this is a summer which lasts for ever; that every month in the year, without interruption, the dark crests of the great cocoanut-palms are covered with their heavy fruit; that this red soil produces incessantly, that it is always bringing forth these swarms of great flowers, that these trees have always the same green and supple magnificence. They crowd each other and are all entangled; there is not a suggestion of the regular, slow growth of European trees. These cocoanut-palms look fresh and soft, like enormous annuals, like some giant cereal,—frail, bending, soaked with sap,—which has grown out of all measure in a hot night of June. Some spring to a very great height, lifting far above the others, with a flexible curve, a strong, graceful impulse, their lofty crest of leaves, spread wide in the warm atmosphere.

And the red road goes on and on, between lustrous heaps of drooping palms, masses of dark vegetation, from which the great sword-like leaves, springing out, flash with green light. Here and there are large ponds of black water—water which is almost invisible, so distinctly and perfectly is the surrounding vegetation reflected in it. Broad bands of pink lotus trail over this water, and seem no more real than the green of the palms' reflection. Here and there, gleaming white, far within a fabulous garden, some handsome villa, crowned with palm-trees—its galleries, verandas, balustrades, steps, all loaded with enchanted flowers. Timid, frail, the Cinhalese glide past, a delicate, gentle race, with masses of ebony-black hair worn long like a woman's, a race made languid by perpetual summer and the constant moist sunlight. They move slowly, their serious and tranquil faces, strangely exotic, expressing an uncomprehended soul—the soul formed by this world so remote from our own.

Going by train to Kandy, on the way I made the acquaintance of a Cinhalese gentleman. Very civilised, this gentleman—altogether correct in his tweed coat with a gardenia in his button-hole, only that his legs were sheathed in a very narrow white petticoat. His physiognomy almost European—like an Italian, but more delicate, feminine, and sunburnt : features, bony and salient; a strong lustrous beard, black and curly.

After fifteen minutes of silence, conversation begins as in a European railway carriage. He offers me a match and remarks that the weather is very warm. A sentence as to the temperature is, in English countries, the indispensable preliminary rite by which human beings enter into communication with each other. After this, in a few very definite words, he gives me information concerning the population of the island, its government, its religions. As he talks, I feel how deep is here the English stamp : he speaks the language with singular purity, without the least accent. He is a Christian, a lawyer, a member of the legislative council. His disdainful pity for "the ignorance and idolatry" of the poor Cinhalese peasant is worthy of an English colonist. But, in fifty years, he says, all this will be changed ; the railways have already done much good ; before them, the savage country retreats. "At Colombo, we hope to found a great university, like that at Bombay or Benares, and later, when we are worthy of it, to have our parliament—a national assembly elected by suffrage of various grades ; all this, of course, by degrees, and without separation from the great British Empire, from England, to whom we owe our entrance into the world of civilisation." He adds that he is "Aryan"; this is as clear and certain to him as it is certain and clear to me that I am French; consequently he esteems himself the equal of any European; and certainly he is the superior of many Europeans in intelligence, education, and manners.

But he is somewhat too English; it is too evident that to him the Englishman is the ideal model of humanity. A copy so perfect is not natural. And then all this European display swears at his white petticoat and at certain Asiatic hints in his physiognomy. Naturally, one prefers the Chinese with his pigtail and his blue robe to the Japanese in frockcoat and Derby hat. One is distrustful at the astonishing address with which individuals of yellow or black skin imitate the European; and cannot but question whether the imitation goes at all below the surface, whether the depths do not still remain mysteriously Mongol or Negro. Certainly this man does his best to surprise me, with his air of knowing the world, his stiff manner, the nonchalant slowness of movement with which he takes an Egyptian cigarette from his case of yellow tortoiseshell.

It is amusing, this little railway upon which my friend, the Cinhalese lawyer, counts to bring civilisation into the depths of the palm forests; a pretty plaything, a nice little toy railway, not very likely to alarm the eternal vegetation of the equator.

The engine burns no vile black coal, but fragrant woods. We glide along under great trees whose leafy tops make a green arch above the track. There are charming stations which have but slight resemblance to a French *gare*, little cabins all pink and blue with climbing flowers and hidden under great glossy shrubs. There is no restaurant, but slender, bronzed *epheboi*, in bright-coloured robes, pass, slow and smiling, holding out baskets filled with pineapples, mangoes, bananas in pink clusters, or sometimes yellow young cocoanuts which they open adroitly with three strokes of a hatchet, that you may drink out of the nut its cool and perfumed milk.

We pass through low lands, damp under the interminable marshy forest. The earth is a vegetable slime which produces unweariedly these multitudes of great, wild, primitive trees. The light never strikes through them; their sombre verdure reflects itself in the blackness of melancholy pools of water. The imprisoned air sleeps heavily among these crowded trunks. Their feet in the tepid water, their heads in the blazing sunshine, the trees spring out of a thicket of colossal brakes, interwoven, gripped fast by tropical climbing plants. Within, one may conjecture what must be the dense humming and the furious whirring of myriads of insects—the violent, primitive life as of the first geologic ages, when, after the great rainy periods, organic life came out of the ground upon the summons of the torrid sun.

We cross the Kelanya Ganga, a brown river flowing between tall green bamboos; then there is an up grade, and almost instantly the landscape changes. We emerge at last from the oppressive virgin forest, and enter a wild garden, intersected with cool, open rice swamps, starred with flowers — the fragrant flowers of the champak and frangipani—a garden of delights, where rocks repose under tall, quivering ferns, where little mossy huts, crouching beneath the Cinhalese greenery, are almost hidden from sight; an Eden, where parrots cleave the air like arrows of light, and great butterflies seem flying flames; where the trees are loaded with golden fruit, and the noble luminous palms hold up green transparencies against the sky. Sometimes roads, like red ribbons, are seen, amid this splendour of flowers; and a peculiar warm fragrance, like the perfume of a greenhouse, arises from the purple earth.

Very near us, as we pass, half hidden by a curtain of climbing plants, two lofty, dark masses, dull-coloured like rock, move, and I perceive two elephants. Peaceful, imperturbable, their great heads drooping, sweeping the ground with their pendant trunks, their big feet spread out softly in the red dust, they move along as if asleep, cradling with their monotonous motion their drivers, who seem also sleeping. Why is it so impressive, the sudden vision of these monsters framed in this equatorial scenery? Is it because they are at home in these thickets, because we know that over there, beyond the mountains, their kind wander at liberty—because they make part of this world, are the living manifestation of this nature, like the palm-trees?

We go on ascending, now along the edge of the rock, making a circuit around steep declivities. At this point vegetation is tamer, and it is possible for man to struggle with it : the plantations of coffee and cocoa begin. We are now on the edge of an immense amphitheatre, sinking beneath us to a depth of several thousand feet clothed with palm-trees and gigantic ferns—a misty amphitheatre, a shadowy valley which traverses half the island, extending as far as Colombo. In its gloomy depths there are the same primitive damp forests—those impenetrable forests from which comes a mysterious sound of life. But beyond, across this valley, the Cinhalese mountains lift their summits to the sky, the old sacred summits, of which all the religions of the island dream ; the crests of barren rock, lifted toward the sun, victorious, at last enfranchised from the weight of all this vegetation.

We reach Kandy, the old native city, the ancient capital of the Cinhalese kings. The Cinhalese kings ! The words have a singular charm. Do they not evoke an impossible, enchanting fairyland, a little court, all fanciful as ever poet dreamed of ? The old palace is there, on the edge of a lake of black water, under tall palm-trees.

All around the little city, sleeping at the foot of low hills, the happy roads wander among flowers.

Near the palace, on the shore of the black lake, wherein swans mirror their white splendour, is a Buddhist temple, an old, strange temple, somewhat Chinese of aspect, with its conical roofs, its rotund pavilions, its carved balustrades, its doors guarded by monsters—a grotesque, outlandish edifice, all white under the thick shadow of the trees. I know not why I had so much trouble in believing that this was a temple. At the first glance, you suspect, you feel, that an Egyptian mosque is a sacred spot. But the Semitic world is near our own, and interpenetrates it. This Cinhalese world is completely separate from us, and has always been so. It is impossible to understand it by sympathy, to discover the habitual mental condition of the race which reproduces itself under these palms, whose vague aspirations are expressed by these architectural forms and by daily offerings of flowers to the smiling Buddha.

Whence come they, and what do they signify, these three formidable monsters grimacing upon the portico ? And of what are they thinking, all day long, these monks who wander over the marble pavements ? Barefooted, with shaven heads, one bare arm emerging from the great yellow robe which drapes them, they glide along the passages ; there are five or six, going noiselessly past, lighting the inner darkness with the soft gleam of their saffron-coloured garments. They smile mysteriously, with a gentle seriousness that is indescribable.

The monk who is my guide conducts me into the great central courtyard, to the sacred fig-tree which consecrated the monastery. It is a scion of the tree Bo, which, for five years, sheltered the meditations of the divine Sakya-Muni. With a slow bend of the head, the monk gave me a leaf of this tree ; at the moment I seemed to read the meaning of his face : the pallid face of a vegetarian, quiet and refined, the prominent forehead, the intelligent, close-shut lips—yet always with the same half-smile, so serious and tranquil.

Silent, they wander among perpetual flowers, in the shadow of the giant bamboos, fed with the few grains of rice that they receive from charity, in the cool darkness of the marble corridors, at the foot of the serene image of the great Buddha : very different are these from the men who, at this moment, with anxious eyes and wrinkled foreheads, jostle each other in the fogs of Bond Street, or on the slippery pavements of Paris.

What is there under this immutable smile ? The Buddhist priest, Sri Smangala, superior of the monastery of Kandy, a very wise and very learned man, who is interested in our Europe, and has the opinion that, with their positivism, their psychology, and their ethics, our thinkers are not far from the doctrines of Buddha, has had the kindness to converse with me for a half-hour. He indicates to me certain books, and gives me an idea of the life of these monks. But, after all, we can only see the outside ; it is impossible to penetrate their souls.

There are two classes of monks, the novices (*samanera*) or mendicants, properly so called ; and the elders (*sramana*), those who can control their wills. To attain the mastery over one's self, which is the grand aim, the monk follows the precepts laid down in the *Pittri Mokkha*, the oldest of the sacred books of Buddhism, which is admitted, even by the severest criticism, to date from the year 350 B.C.

A monk is allowed to possess eight things : three robes, a girdle, a wooden bowl to receive alms, a razor, a needle, and a filter to remove from what he drinks the particles of organic matter, which are held sacred, because they have life. In the monastery all the minor rules concerning this life of poverty are strictly observed. The novice rises before daylight, washes his garment, sweeps the corridors of the temple and the ground around the sacred fig-tree, then draws the water for the day's use, and filters it. He then withdraws into a solitary place, and meditates; having placed flowers before the sacred tree, he thinks upon the virtues of Buddha and upon his own failings; after this, he takes his bowl and accompanies his superior, who goes out to beg. They ask for nothing, but they stand silently before the door. Returning, the novice washes his master's feet, washes his wooden bowl, boils his rice; and thinks upon the goodness and charity of Buddha. After an hour he lights a lamp and begins to study, copies manuscripts, or else, perhaps, sitting at the feet of his superior, receives instruction from him, and confesses to him the faults of the day.

The elder monks, enfranchised from manual labour, give more time to meditation; not to prayer, for the Buddhist does not invoke aid from the Divinity. To escape from suffering, he depends upon himself only, using the method which Spinoza and the Stoics also recommend, namely, to forget the fleeting self in a consideration of the universe of existences. This universe he contemplates in five meditations, of which the first is called *Maitri-bhavana*, or reflection upon love. Thinking upon all creatures that live, and reflecting what happiness would be his if he were himself free from all sorrow, passion, or evil desire, he wishes to all beings this felicity. Then, toward his enemies, remembering only their good actions, he strives in all sincerity to wish them the same happiness that he would desire for himself.

The second meditation (*Karuna-bhavana*) is that of pity. Thinking of all beings who suffer, and endeavouring to conceive their sufferings, he seeks to awaken in himself the grief that others feel, and to have sincere pity for them.

The third is the meditation upon joy (*Muditabhavana*). Thinking of all people who are happy, or believe themselves to be so, the monk represents to himself the happiness of others, and rejoices in their joy.

The fourth meditation (*Asubha-bhavana*) is upon impurity. Thinking upon the wickedness and the pollution of the body, the monk says to himself that this is all fugitive as the foam of the sea, that all this exists only from the alternating succession of births and deaths, and that this succession is only an appearance.

Lastly, comes the meditation upon serenity (*Upeksha-bhavana*). Thinking of all things that are esteemed to be good or to be evil, and that are evanescent: power and dependence; love and hate; wealth and poverty; fame and ignominy; youth and beauty, old age and disease;—he contemplates them all with invincible indifference, with absolute serenity.

There are in this monastery a hundred and twenty monks; it is a learned, and moreover a legal, institution, respected as in old times some great abbey, Cîteaux or St. Germain, with us. I visited the library, a quiet hall with a domed roof, where the palm-leaf manuscripts are kept, enveloped in linen. In a corner some Japanese novices—pilgrims and students from the other end of the Buddhist world —were reading. I was shown a beautiful red book, containing three *pitakas*, or sacred writings, from the Buddhists of the South. On the first page were these words:

" *To the very reverend Sri Weligama, Superior of the Monastery of Kandy, in token of respect,*

"EDWARD, PRINCE OF WALES."

About five o'clock the heat of the sun has abated. I quit the temple, eager to lose myself in this equatorial nature. Nature is the one thing to be seen here, and, in the presence of her grandeur, men and customs fail to interest. Whence comes this all-powerful attraction? Is it because our remote ancestors, the first beings who had the human form, made their appearance in a world like this, when the continents were covered by all this tropical growth? Is it that their instincts, asleep for centuries, awaken in us, at sight of things which were familiar to them?

I follow a deserted road, between hedges starry

with blue, yellow, and red flowers—enormous, splendid flowers, with stiff, satiny petals, growing wild here, but more magnificent than a king's conservatories could show. And out of this sumptuous parterre spring tall, supple stems, caoutchouc, Chinese bamboo, with palm leaves ten feet long. At the left, below the road, a grove of cocoanut-trees extends down the hill, and the straight, close-crowded stems, each crowned with its great cluster of stiff leaves, is like an army of young men, lordly and primitive, their heads bristling with great savage plumes. They are there by thousands, the axils of their branches laden with young cocoanuts, which must be very tender and cool to eat. Nothing gives a better idea of force than the way these rigid, parallel columns spring up into the air. The violence of the organising power which raised them out of the soil, the suction of earth and water by their roots, the swarming multitudes of them brought forth in this tropical heat—all this is very impressive to the imagination. Other trees are loaded with a green scaly fruit, as large as one's head; this, I recognise as the breadfruit. Here are also mango-trees, the nutmeg, the cinnamon, the mahogany-tree, impenetrable thickets of unknown essences, whence rise in sheaves twenty kinds of palm-trees, not stiff, solitary, dusty, like the Egyptian palm, but supple, glossy, grassy—these children of the humid equator. You have but to step on the green grass along the roadside, and at once it curls up, withers, grows yellow in great spots. This intensity of vegetable life is something marvellous. It quivers in these sensitive plants; it stiffens in these tropical creepers, which drop from the highest tree-tops to the ground in tight-stretched curtains of green ; it blazes in these scarlet leaves and in the gleam of poisonous flowers amid the verdure. Amid all this vegetation run mad, the red road goes on. Below, among the pillared cocoanut-palms, here and there I catch a glimpse of a broad yellow river running with great rapidity; and in the distance, northward, drowned in a tide of greyish clouds, is the vapoury outline of mountains. This is the virgin land of Ceylon, where still roam the wild elephant, akin to the vanished mastodon, and the *Veddah*, the last survivor of the prehistoric man.

Some Cinhalese go by—the men wearing the long skirt, girt about the waist, the rest of the figure nude, the hair fastened up in a knot, slender and bronzed ; the women, gracefully draped, with lifted arm half-bent, shelter the head by a great stiff leaf used as a parasol. One, a Greek torso, with Aryan features, her bronze skin lustreless against the crimson of her short drawers, carries a jar upon her shoulder.

A family returning from hunting go by in Indian file. At its head a man, in red skirt, a long, slender gun in his hand, walks with short, timid steps. The woman follows him. Behind trot two little boys, quite naked, very frail-looking, and one holds the spoils by its claw—a poor little yellow parrot, whose pretty head hangs down, the eyes closed in death. It is a happy and peaceful population which lives under these lofty palms, finding food at hand in the cocoanut and the breadfruit. A family possesses a cocoanut grove : they live in its shelter ; they live upon its fruit. They go half-clad, graceful and slow of motion, smiling as you pass them, perpetually combing their hair with a comb of yellow tortoiseshell. At every fountain basin the bathers are sporting in the water, or lounging under the trees in the green shadow of the foliage. A happy race, an idle existence ; they are Tennyson's lotus-eaters. Their religion is worthy of themselves, simple and calm. It does not lead to passionate emotions, like Christianity ; nor to overwhelming metaphysical meditations, tyrannical rites, and foolish ceremonies, like the Indian Brahmanism. Without doubt, there is in Buddhism much high metaphysics with which the Cinhalese priests are familiar ; but they do not worry the people with this. To live peaceably, and in the evening to come and bow before the smiling Buddha, and throw at his feet the great flowers of the frangipani : their religion requires nothing of them—nothing more than this. Man is very gentle here, very languid, dominated by this overwhelming nature, by the fiery sunshine and the overflowing vegetation. He makes no revolt, no struggle against the uncaring or rival development of the inanimate around him. There is no tragic conflict, no "struggle for existence," none of that manifestation of the human will by which man asserts his supremacy and takes his place as a force, in the presence of the forces of the material world. Here all destinies are alike ; they all live here among the flowers, feebler than they, half asleep in the warm air and the enervating perfume.

At last the road turns, and leads back to the town, lying along the edge of an immense plateau, and always under the shadow of enormous trees. On one side, a dense, shadowy jungle, where monkeys abound; on the left, the misty valley, terminating in the far distance with phantom outlines of mountain crests and peaks. And now, suddenly, without any twilight, night comes on; and forests and horizons alike disappear in the sudden darkness, like some luminous dream which melts away all at once.

Now the equatorial stars come out. There is a great silence, with a few plaintive sounds out of the invisible forests, and the buzzing of insects. Moments like these are loaded with an indescribable, pleasurable melancholy; certain successions of sounds make the heart heavy, one knows not why—traverse the soul with a strange, deep thrill. Suddenly, one feels so remote, so lost, in the indifferent tranquillity of nature! One feels himself detached from the group to which a human being belongs: his country, friends, family; the illusion that life makes to each of us is unmade, and the man stands alone, a creature for a moment flung out of the darkness and driven hither and thither upon the surface of the incomprehensible.

Millions of stars—stars that seem alive—quiver in the spaces overhead. Below, the silent silhouettes, the giant phantoms of great ferns and unfamiliar trees, seem like a dream. The air is full of the humming of the great tropical insects. Fireflies flit in the darkness, and you turn your head to listen, as you catch a far-distant, almost imperceptible, sound of barbaric music, a strangely-rhythmed noise of trumpets and gongs telling of an offering of flowers in some temple in a remote village.

As I draw near Kandy the road becomes populous. Men and women are crowding into the town. From afar, in the silence, the singular Buddhist chant calls them across the jungles, and they come from their remote little dwellings, scattered in the thickets under the tall palm-trees.

Moving rapidly among the silent bands of the flower-laden worshippers, I cross the city, almost invisible in the dense darkness. There is no other sound than the throbbing of the gongs which fills the air. Beside the black lake, upon the great portico, the three monsters are always watching, and the entrance to the gardens is guarded by priests, who silently receive the offerings. Passing under a silver grating, we come into the darkness of a great hall, where small sacred lamps throw mysterious gleams. Perfumes arise from a hundred censers and spread in bluish clouds, which hang motionless overhead; and this heavy, stupefying incense gives to the scene a certain unreality and character as of a dream. Here and there, half visible in the obscurity, there are formidable silhouettes of enormous Buddhas, Buddhas sitting, Buddhas reposing, in the midst of flowers.

We ascend a dark staircase; on either side are obscure frescos of demons confusedly struggling amid flames; above, standing behind a silver balustrade, priests receive the flowers which the worshippers lay upon a large table. In front of this silent multitude a very handsome youth stands motionless, his arms filled with a great heap of fragrant jasmine. He offers the flowers, then bows several times before the image, and then stands, half bending forward, his hands crossed on his breast, smiling, with his beautiful curved lips and long, lustrous eyes, a strange smile, mystic and wild. There is an oppressive silence, suddenly broken by the deep vibration of the tomtom and trumpet, and the Asiatic chant rising from below. In the faint light of the sacred lamps, the priests, indistinct, silent, standing behind the flowers, are solemn and hieratic. To see this serious, effeminate crowd, thus moving about in the dim, perfumed vapour, to see them slowly perform the prescribed gestures of the rite, seems like some consecrated mystery of remote ages, some Eleusinian initiation.

Quite in the background, in a solitary tabernacle behind the priests, an inviolate retreat, a great figure of crystal, vague in outline, casting no shadow, sits, with crossed legs. And its transparency seems as that of a phantom, a pure spirit, enfranchised from matter; this is a symbolic image of him who, by the intensity of his meditation, breaks the bonds of flesh and of desire. Dominating the crowd, he seems superior to the restlessness of humanity, and the eternal smile of his translucent lips tells he has entered into eternal peace.

The more I observe this country and these men, the better I understand, it seems to me, this religion and this system of ethics. The point of departure is in the human being : the fatigue, the crushing load, an immense need of rest and quietude, in presence of natural phenomena that are so violent, disproportionate, and full of change, where all visible things undergo incessant renewal, are for ever springing into existence and for ever perishing. What is said to-day by our great European thinkers has been taught by the Buddhist sages for the last three centuries. Nothing *is*, they say ; all *becomes ;* the world is but a current of ephemeral appearances ; there is nothing stable in it, and nothing permanent except change itself. The earth, the sky, the twenty-eight *inferni*, demons themselves, and the inferior worlds which they inhabit, all is for ever flowing past like the waters of a river ; or, more truly, is coming and going like the diverse colours of a flame, which springs up, becomes intense, decreases, is extinguished. After this one, another, and then another ; and so on, through a series in perpetually recurrent cycles. The series is eternal ; it had no beginning, and will have no end.

In this universe, what is man ? A something that thinks, but, like all the rest of things, nothing more than a sum of forces, united for a time, but condemned presently to separate ; a collection of faculties and tendencies, a series of images, ideas, fancies, wishes, emotions, which are transitory, while their order for a time subsists, as the form

c

and structure of an organised body endures through the perishing and reconstructing of the molecules which compose it. Nothing in man is stable, neither the incidents which collectively and successively, according to a certain law, constitute his personality, nor that law itself, which changes slowly with his growth and his decline. There are five elements (*skandhas*) whose cohesion makes the individual, and the Buddhist shows in detail that no one of these elements is a permanent substance. The first comprises the material qualities (extent, solidity, colour); these are like the foam, which slowly is born, then vanishes. The second includes the sensations; these are like bubbles dancing on the surface of the water. In the third, perceptions and judgments are like the vague mists of noonday. In the fourth, the moral and mental tendencies "are like the plantain stem, which has no strength or solidity." To conclude, thoughts, the fifth, are spectres, illusions of magic.

"O mendicants!" said Gautama, "in whatever manner the different teachers regard the soul, they imagine it to be one of the five elements, or to be the sum of them all. Thus, O mendicants! the man who is not converted, and who does not understand the law of the converted, sometimes considers the soul as identical with the material qualities, or as possessing them, or as containing them, or as residing in them; sometimes as identical with sensation, or as containing it, or as residing in it," and so on, as to the other three elements. Conceiving the soul, therefore, in one or other of these ways, he reaches the idea : I am. From sensation, for example, the ignorant or sensual man derives the notion : I am ; this *I* exists. I shall be or not be, I shall have or shall not have material qualities, I shall have or not have ideas. " But the wise disciple of converted men, though he possesses the five organs of the senses, being freed from ignorance, has attained to knowledge. For this reason the ideas : I am, this *I* exists, I shall be or shall not be, no longer present themselves to his mind."

Descartes has said : *Cogito, ergo sum.* The Buddha would have said : " I think, therefore I am not." For what is thought but a series of changes, a succession of different events ? According to modern psychologists it is nothing else. A mechanism, which Taine in France and Stuart Mill in England have studied, creates in us the illusion of the *I*-substance, the most pernicious of all, Buddhists say —the principal snare laid for us by Maya, the great Tempter ; for this is the tie which attaches us to things, the great mirage which plucks us from immobility and indifference, and flings us into action and drives us onward. Buddhism calls this heresy, the heresy of individualism (*sakkaya ditthi*).

Once admit that there is nothing in the world but a flow of appearances, that neither in ourselves, nor outside of ourselves, anything is lasting, and conduct becomes clear ; the man recognises as an illusion this *I* which seemed to him so important. He is at once enfranchised ; he no longer aspires to continue this *I;* he ceases to make effort, or to desire; he has lost the thirst for life, and is thus set free from suffering. For whence comes suffering? Precisely from these events which constitute personal existence: birth, old age, illness, decrepitude, death. And why are these events suffering? Because the illusion of the *I*, whence comes the will to live and to persist in existence, creates desire and fear, makes us repulse old age and illness and death, and desire their opposites. Uproot from us this love of being, and, ceasing to resist, or act, or think, escaping the universal law of change, we shall become insensible to suffering, which proceeds from change. "He who conquers this contemptible thirst of being, suffering quits him, as drops of water slip off the lotus leaf." There follows an enumeration of the ways that lead to this condition of perfection: the first, which destroys the heresy of individualism and the belief in the necessity of rites and ceremonies; the second, which destroys all passion, all hate, all illusion; the third, which removes the last traces of self-love; the fourth, or lofty path of the *arahats*, that is to say, of men enfranchised by intuition, who have ceased to aspire to any existence, material or immaterial.

Arriving at this point, the man has given up himself; he no longer gravitates toward himself; he is no longer a centre of attraction, an egoistic force labouring to persist. He can give himself to others; and charity, pity for another's sufferings, penetrates his heart. "As a mother, at the risk of her own life, defends her son, her only son, let a man cultivate a boundless love for all that exists, for the entire world; let this love extend around him, above him, below him, free from the rival sentiment of self-interest: let him persist firmly in this condition of mind during all his waking hours, whether he is standing or sitting, in action or in repose." "His senses are at peace. He is like a well-trained horse: he is freed from pride, washed from the pollution of ignorance, insensible to the incitements of the flesh." It appears that the gods themselves envy a fate like this. "He whose conduct is upright is like the broad earth, immovable; like the columns which sustain a portico, steadfast; calm as a lake of crystal." For him there is no further birth. "Tranquil is the mind, tranquil are the words and acts of him who is enfranchised by wisdom. They aspire not to a future life; the allurement of living having disappeared, and no new desire arising in their hearts, they, the wise, become extinct, as a lamp to which no new oil is supplied." This is the supreme felicity. Having sounded the depths of all things, Sakya-Muni, like the Brahmas, his predecessors, found nothing substantial. All substance that he touched melted under his hand, and his embrace enfolded only the empty air. Everywhere gleamed illusive phantasmagoria, everywhere events whirled and fled away. Nothing was permanent; let us cease, therefore, to wish to be permanent ourselves. Nature deceives the ignorant, to attain her ends; but the wise man refuses to be duped by her. He escapes from the incessant motion of appearances to take refuge in the calm of nothingness. He has made a void in his own mind, nothing moves within him, and if his lips stir, it is only in a smile of charity and compassion for the sad human tumult.

Such are the characteristic features of this Buddhist religion, whose rites I witnessed in the faintly-lighted temple near the black lake. Inertia, a condition of being at peace, a blessed quietude, an indifference of the will, a numbness of the personality, gentleness—all these Buddhist virtues are visible among these Cinhalese of the interior, this gracious people who just now bent silently before the sacred image, ignorant of effort, of revolt, and of despair, smiling and at rest, among the flowers. Whether their tranquillity and languor come to them from their religion, or whether their religion only gives expression to tendencies in them which surrounding nature has established, they are true Buddhists. They are walking in the first of the paths of salvation ; above them, these priests who receive the flowers, impassive behind the silver railings, these ascetic mendicants, with close-shut lips and intellectual brows, are sages walking in the second and third paths, victorious over passion and hate and illusion. But the Buddhists tell us no man has attained to the highest path, no man has reached the lofty, serene regions, the calm of Nirwana, except the Master, whose pale, expressionless face is faintly seen in the dimness, above the priests and the worshippers, with eyes nearly closed, amid moving clouds of perfume.

In the morning it was a great surprise on awaking to find myself here, the red road in front, and the tiny houses crouching among the verdure of the hills. At this early hour, all things have a singular glitter, a wet, fresh lustre. Silvery mists cling to the hillsides, and softly enwrap the terraced palm-trees, which rise out of the vapour, dripping with dew and shining with virgin brilliancy. Not a person is to be seen on the road leading to the Peradinya Gardens; there is only this fragrant vegetation, as of a newly-created paradise in which man has not yet appeared.

At a bend of the road a bridge of black wood appears, and I stand still in wonder. Under the open sky, between two walls of solid verdure, a muddy, lustrous river moves with slow current. There is not a wave, not a ripple, not a shiver on its surface; the heavy water moves as if solid, its brown lustre cut by strong, motionless shadows. On both sides the luxuriance of wet vegetation: at the left noble palm-trees, rising in terraces, lustrous, mighty, and regular, thrice royal in their height, their beauty, and their glossy foliage; at the right, thick clumps of trees, verdant walls of bamboo, and tropical climbers, a luxuriance of green and supple things, which spring out of the muddy soil, crowding, crushing each other to get to the light, and then falling back in a confused mass, spreading itself out in the blackness of the shadow which all this vegetation casts upon the river. And all along, so far as the lustrous curve can be seen, the same display of useless strength carelessly lavished to overflowing, the same furious outburst of life.

Not far distant are the Peradinya Gardens, where I spend the day, dining alone on a little rice and some cocoanuts in the hut of a Cinhalese keeper. One can walk for many leagues in this place, meeting no human being, yet still conscious of a certain order, a plan in this marvellous, wild garden. It is the paradise of some Eastern tale, designed, inhabited, by invisible genii, far from the real, terrestrial life. Humming-birds in endless variety, a little winged world, sparkle in the magnificence of this solitude. There are wide lawns where tropical plants can grow freely and attain their full size; there are stiff avenues of lofty trees, which shoot up, shining and metallic, their foliage, a single cluster of palm leaves, a hundred and twenty feet from the ground; there are ferns of improbable shades, blue ferns subtle as vapours; there are leaves as delicate as dream vegetation—green lace, like a cobweb, varieties of Adiantum, a very fairies' hair. At the end of an avenue of banians there are giant caoutchoucs extending their enormous branches so far that, unable to be supported by the parent trunk, they drop to the ground, take root, and form new trees. In every direction their monstrous roots, thrown out from the ground, rise, in rough vertebræ four feet high, and spread to a great distance with powerful, sinuous motion. It is like molten rock, a radiation of cooled lava from some primeval crater long extinct.

At last I reach the triumph, the apotheosis, so to speak, of the island's vegetation. On the edge of the gardens, beside the slow-moving, yellowish water of a *ganga*, there is a sheaf of bamboos a hundred feet in circuit. They are crowded together, smothering each other, each one as large as a European tree. The hard stems, bluish and glossy, in joints two feet long, perfectly round, are gorged with water. Some, spotted with green, seem to have been poisoned. They grow so crowded that only the outside stems are visible; the others, covered and repressed, spring straight up in darkness. With a supple movement, at the height of a hundred feet, they separate, spread apart in the form of a vase, and are lost in a great rustling mass of dark leafage. This gloomy sheaf has something actually sinister in its aspect; it seems to be an upspringing of venomous sap. Really, you feel yourself overcome with terror in the presence of a gigantic force whose outburst nothing can arrest. It is impossible to describe this crowd of trunks, packed close against each other, the violence of their impetus, the lithe slenderness of the lofty stems. The life is strong and simple in these giants of the tropical flora. In June and July they grow a foot a day. Now, even in November, the sap is all in ebullition, and the organic work goes on in a tumult of eagerness; this is quite different from the slow growth of our oak-trees in Europe, built up, cell after cell, by the deliberate hand of centuries. These bamboos are big grasses; they have the brilliancy and suppleness of ferns, as they spring up impetuously from the deep soil toward the creating sun.

November 12.

Yesterday, on the railway, returning from the interior of the island, I met a Hollander; fat, gentle, pale, peaceful of gesture, scanty of speech. Of the Dutch temperament there is left only the phlegm and softness; the sanguine flesh tint has disappeared under the heat. After five minutes he asked me my address, that he might send me some flowers; for my pockets overflowing with roses, jasmines, mimosas, my admiration for the very great size of the floral display on every side, had surprised him. After a time I learned that my man is a native of Ceylon, that he has tea plantations in the mountain, and lives, with his family, at Colombo. To-day I dine with him. His bungalow, situated in the cinnamon gardens, is like a villa of some rich old Roman: deliciously bright and cool, immense halls separated by partitions of fragrant woods, carved and cut in fretwork; great wicker *chaises longues*, where one may recline all day with cigarette or book. The children pretty, but singularly pallid, a translucid, waxen tint, fined down and enfeebled by the climate; a household of servants, who seem very much beloved; parents and children speak Cinhalese to them.

After breakfast we loiter in the garden, where grow freely the rare flowers of our greenhouses, and the most beautiful Cinhalese palms. As I broke a blade of some large grass-like plant, a jet of sap burned my hand. This shows the heat and activity of Cinhalese vegetation.

I am obliged to go; to-night we shall be at sea. I desired to see again the calm and serious eyes of the monks and the smile of the reclining Buddha, that the recollection might not be lost at once; accordingly I ended my last day in the temple of Colombo.

In the evening, while the day was dying, I went as far as the beach of Mount Lavinia, a solitary shore bordered by a tall, dark forest of cocoanut-trees, which suggests a thought of little savage, desolate islands upon the equator's line, lost in the vast expanse of waters. In the distance, roughened by the wind outside, the sea was blue, the vast Indian Ocean, all alive, full of ardour and force, foaming upon the horizon in sudden and silent patches of white. The big waves coming in upon the red land broke with dull, heavy sound, and amid the monotony of this tumult, from time to time, I heard the sad rustling of the tall cocoanut-trees.

CHAPTER III

PONDICHÉRY   CALCUTTA

November 16.

WE resume the sea life : long enervating days upon the tranquil water, under the same sky, pale with excess of light ; long nights on deck, under the tropical stars ; and then, a weariness of this monotony.

One morning we awake in the harbour of Pondichéry. Natives, nude and black, each with his big turban on, have come paddling out to us. Rapidly resuming their costume of ceremony (which is only a handkerchief), and climbing by the port-holes like a band of lively ants, they seize upon us and hurry us into their skiffs. They ply their paddles rapidly, their eyes shining with delight, and utter enthusiastic cries, in which suddenly we recognise French words :

"*Hurrah pour papa!   Hurrah pour maman! Hurrah pour le bon voyage!*"

This is all they know of our language, the big, savage children. This ignorance does not prevent them, I understand, from possessing the franchise, and voting, with all the dignity of free citizens. The high-priest of the pagoda comes to an agreement with the governor, and the people vote under his orders, as they would perform a rite, a religious ceremony akin to the periodical procession of the sacred images in their chariots.

A great crowd on the pier. We bring with us a high functionary of the Republic. The military forces of French India, the three hundred Sepoys that Great Britain tolerates, are here, drawn up in double rank, enchanted at playing soldier, very much pleased with their brilliant uniforms. With many blows from the butt-end of guns the crowd of curious natives is kept off; the whites, however, pass freely under the arches of triumph on which appear official welcomes and acclamations. Poor, white population of Pondichéry, poor Frenchmen, born so far away, posterity of gallant ancestors who established themselves here when France was a famous power on Indian soil, and are now so forgotten, so remote! I notice descendants of old colonial families, and nothing is more striking than to discover in them the features and the expression of our race. They seem marvellously provincial, behind the times, with a kind of fatigue, effeminacy, enfeeblement, sometimes an appearance of being withered. Everything here seems like a little French provincial town, very remote from the centre, yet living only by the few drops of life distributed from their own centre, the fatuous sub-prefecture, where everything is according to rule, tiresome, old-fashioned. This place is much more remote from Paris than Carpentras or Landerneau.

Meantime the high functionary disembarks. The notables receive him; there are prolonged presentations and official smiles. Very pompously, a native personage bends before him, much entangled in his white robes, loaded with jewels, very stout and heavy of motion, his little eyes blinking in his fat, dull Brahman's face. He leans with dignity upon his silver cane, an heirloom with which his family was honoured one day, when, bullets having given out, his ancestor offered ingots of gold wherewith to bombard the English laying siege to Pondichéry.

More presentations, addresses, shaking of hands. Now the functionary of the Republic, attended by his secretaries in black coats, advances at the head of the procession, passes under the triumphal arches, and the French army of the three hundred Sepoys marches after. Very touching, and slightly comic in its exotic setting, is this ceremony, which recalls our distributions of prizes, official inaugurations of monuments, and electoral rounds made by ministers.

The city is agreeable to behold, bright and clean. Everywhere this red Indian soil, and perfumes from unseen sources. The roads stretch away in straight lines, bordered by palm-trees, and constantly traversed by little striped squirrels raising little clouds of dust. We are already far distant from Ceylon; this vegetation has something precise and well regulated about it. This avenue of palm-trees was no doubt the same ten years ago that it is to-day; there is nothing of the soft undulation of rapid growth here.

The greatest delight of the eye here is to observe

this multitude of women moving about, so simply and superbly draped. With their erect bearing, the shoulders thrown back, the head carrying a copper jar, their outlines are truly statuesque. Notwithstanding the brilliancy of colour, it is a world that makes one think of ancient Greece; the same plastic attitudes, the same tranquillity of gesture, the same outdoor life, and the same small houses built of earth, low, cool, white, square, devoid of furniture, where women sit in the shadow and spin.

At two miles' distance from Pondichéry we come to the pagoda of Villianur; and we no longer think of Greece. Above the village—twenty wretched hovels of dried mud, twenty huts of savages, within whose shade black figures with bestial heads are drowsing—rises an indescribable something, a bluish heap of swarming figures, a confused pyramid of porcelain monsters, grimacing, innumerable, in serried ranks, one above another. It is hideous and insane, this pagoda roof; it is an imagination of a diseased brain, which, crushed, perverted by the torrid sun, raves in grotesque and horrible visions. And in this heap of shapeless figures, of twisted limbs that writhe about each other, there is not merely the lack of sanity, but there is also a something savage, disturbing, incomprehensible, like the Polynesian idols or the ancient sanguinary Mexican divinities—something that speaks of the old indigenous races which the Aryan conquerors met everywhere in India : mysterious black races that still people this southern part of the peninsula, sending out wandering tribes through the forests of the interior. This character is noticeable in all the architecture of Southern India. Next door to Pondichéry, at Madura and Trichinopoli, it attains its utmost extravagance and strangeness, displaying itself in granite pagodas as large as cities, covering the earth with pillars, heaping up, in gigantic pyramids, gods and goddesses, demons, heroes, monkeys, horses, elephants—a whole world of human and animal forms, which are massed together in most astonishing confusion.

A crowd of black-skinned priests and worshippers came yelping about us, and a hundred hands were greedily stretched out. Some random blows with a stick from my guide, and sadness settled upon their faces, outcries changed to wailing, and the begging hands were extended, clasped in supplication. Quick, some little silver coins to restore joy in this poor black world; and the piteous faces of the Brahmans are overspread with broad smiles of infantile delight! At once they send the crowd away, and consult, with an air of mystery. Two minutes' conference, and then two of the older priests slip away, they vanish into the sanctuary, and return triumphantly, their faces radiant at the surprise they are preparing for us, leading out a troop of bayaderes in full costume. Clad in silks, their noses, ears, arms, and ankles loaded with rings, with languid, alluring gestures, and shiverings of the body and of the finger-tips, they execute an erotic pantomime. Not very seductive, these bayaderes, with their brutish fat faces and thick lips which mark the inferior race. Their look is vacant and almost idiotic, the mouth open in a stupid smile. Evidently the soul is lacking; these black women are too near the animal.

Behind them is the entrance to the sanctuary; we are not allowed to go in; but in the darkness I can discover vague figures of gilded divinities, and an extremely ugly idol in a tabernacle. Idols, bayaderes, pyramids of monsters heaped upon each other, black-skinned worshippers, savage, begging priests, we leave them all with little delay, somewhat confused, not very well comprehending what we have seen.

In the evening, returning to Pondichéry, I observe the statue of Dupleix. He looks toward the sea, standing, in an attitude of command, bold, imperious, with defiant eyes full of an extraordinary determination and hardihood. "A famous man," says an Englishman, "and one who gave us no end of trouble. And now what good is Pondichéry to you? You oblige us to keep customs officers on the frontier; and all our robbers take refuge with you. What does this colony bring you in?"

"Nothing at all," a Frenchman replied; "but Dupleix must have a statue in India, and he must have it on his own ground."

November 19.

What is this new sea on which we sail to-day, all brown and muddy, with dense, heavy waves? There are no shores on the horizon. As far as the eye can see, quivers, under the clear blue sky, this great mud-coloured circle, shot through with tawny lights. We are entering the mouth of the Hugli; these waters are loaded with earth brought by the Ganges and the Brahmaputra from the plains of Hindustan and the slopes of the Himalaya. About two o'clock in the afternoon the sea begins to be covered with flecks, brown like itself, but motionless, dull, or of a uniform lustre, and in the general glitter the only points that do not sparkle in the sunlight. This is the mud which the river deposits, earth which it casts up from its waters—earth as yet inert, entirely bare, primitive brute matter; but destined to be a source of life in the future, whence will spring tropical jungles with their swarming organisms, their venomous vegetation, their hum of fiery insects, their pestilential marshes. And one recalls to mind that far away, beyond the horizon, along an extent of two hundred miles, this prolific slime is slowly accumulating; in the midst of the barren waters there is silently forming a new bit of Asia.

By degrees a shore appears; but very indistinct, ill defined, a shore of soft mud, only a little above the water, like the earth in early days of creation. Then, there is vegetation: herbaceous at first, gloomy thickets of bamboos and climbing plants; then dense jungles which thrive in an air made pestilential by too rapid vegetable growth and decay,— deadly hotbeds of fermentation where cholera and fever are endemic,—where Nature, left to herself in the absence of man, again essays the soft forms of primitive life, and crocodiles and serpents and giant frogs bask in the tepid mud, and flowers, stimulated by the putrid miasma, climb like flames around the lofty trees. It is a place where, if one were shipwrecked, the river itself would be less dangerous than the jungle with its fevers and its beasts of prey; and so, here and there on the shore there are white towers where sailors who have been cast away can find food and medicine and be out of reach of tigers, while they wait for some passing boat to take them off.

We advance slowly, with infinite precautions. The great river is vehement, and would quickly overturn the boat if, caught for an instant on a sand-bank, she presented her side to the current. We take soundings constantly. The river bed is of moving sands, which the violence of the water displaces, agitates, digs out, heaps up. Now the shores close in, and cultivated lands appear: vast golden harvests, light-coloured rice-fields, noble clusters of shining palms. On the edge of the bank a white file of natives is moving through the tall grass. Upon the river great vessels are passing slowly, powerful steamers, whose destinations are England, and America, and Australia. There are brigs at anchor in great numbers, the splendid sunlight shining upon their poor worn sides, which have the sinuous curve of the waves. They have laboured on their solitary way, lost in the far-off darkness of ocean, racked in all their ribs, lifted on cruel waves, falling into treacherous hollows with heavy shock,—patient hours of obscure suffering. To-day, how peaceful is their sleep upon the shining, rippling surface of the great river!

The activity increases : one feels the nearness of a vast human hive. Heavy lighters go by, laying their broad paunches upon the heavy brown water, careening under the effort of the strained sail, the man at the helm a black figure against the light tint of the sky. The water around us is now yellow, sirupy, and the waves, as they rise in light-coloured, sinuous undulations, seem to glide over the darkness.

A great Liverpool steamer crosses us, high out of the water, five hundred feet long, all black, her huge side rising like an iron fortress. We have a glimpse of an English crowd : anxious-looking faces; men in white flannel; girls with yachting caps; red soldiers.

And then palm-trees again, which are singularly in contrast with great yellow factories and huge smoking chimneys, exactly like those which blacken the *grisaille* of our northern sky. Suddenly, a bend of the river ; a forest of masts appears, and behind them, lofty houses—Calcutta, all white, all glittering in the sunlight.

November 23.

Three days at Calcutta. I have seen nothing, confused by the crowd, overwhelmed by the heat. One thing comes to the surface—the sensation of white ; white light, white houses, the white-clad crowd streaming through the streets. It is to Colombo or Pondichéry as London is to a peaceable country town. By the number of shops, offices, banks, carriages, placards upon the walls, you would think it might be Holborn or the Rue de la Bourse. But in the streets, instead of Europeans in black coats and silk hats, there is a noisy multitude of small and slender Bengalis, wrapped in white muslin, delicate, feminine of feature—not indolent and drowsy as in Ceylon, but active, nervous, rapid, quivering with life. Here, as in London, from the pencil vendors kneeling in a row along the side-walk, to the fat babus reclining in their carriages, all the world is in hot pursuit of money; it is at once apparent that this city is one of the commercial centres, one of the great markets of the world.

Nothing is more grotesque than the *mélange* of Asia and London. At times you might think yourself in the West End, near Hyde Park. The same broad, straight streets, the same monumental houses, the same porticos with Greek columns, the same broad side-walks, the same parks with railings around them, the same English statues at street corners. But, at certain hours, all this is deserted; light fills all the space, and vibrates with a white splendour in the silence. In the active hours, naked men, whose black skins exude moisture from every pore, run about, fighting the dust, flinging water from the leathern sack that they carry under the arm. In offices men work the punkah overhead. At times in summer the shops are shut, the horse-cars stop running, the streets become empty. Upon the whole, activity is artificial here. Nature is too strong for man to be able to forget her, as he does in Belgium or in England; for him to give himself entirely to labour, for him to cover everything with his work. One can be very happy here, but there must be tranquillity and silence, and the green shade of trees — the kind of life natural to the country.

Some expeditions at random in the town. One morning I attempt to penetrate the native quarters. In the narrower streets always the same hurrying crowd of Bengalis, the same thousands of white petticoats, the same thousands of dark, thin, refined faces. From time to time, yellow faces of Chinese, in their blue frocks; and foreign faces—men from Nepaul, from the Dekkan, from Afghanistan. In vain I seek the outskirts of the town, the streets go on; they are crossed by others, they end in new streets, always full of the same fluttering white garments and the same multitude, with its confused noise, its continuous hum as of a hive of bees. And one returns, oppressed by the feeling of this human tide. We are accustomed to say, it is true, that our Europe is but a little corner of the globe, where there has been a local and peculiar development of humanity; we all know that there are other human types; we know that there have been others, just as, beside a certain forest of oaks, there grows a forest of pines; just as, before a certain forest of oaks, there grew a forest of great ferns. But this is merely a cold and abstract idea, void of images and emotions. Here we do indeed perceive the mystery and the diversity of this humanity rising from its deep, obscure springs in millions of undulating waves, all of them ephemeral, born only to disappear, for ever driven out of existence by the incessant afflux of new water, which some blind, imperious effort, we know not what, lifts toward the light. Thrown suddenly into the midst of this teeming Asiatic world, we discover one of these springs, entirely distinct from our own, having never mingled with it, yet equally deep, inexhaustible, copious, and equally grand in its manifestation of the Being who is never weary in diffusing Himself abroad, according to countless types, in all the variety of sentient life.

CHAPTER IV

THE HIMALAYA DARJILING

November 24.

TWENTY-FOUR hours of railway bring us to Darjiling and the chain of the Himalaya. We take the train at the Bengal Northern Station. It is as large as King's Cross or the Gare de Lyon. In the great glazed terminus, trains ready to depart await their passengers; and multitudes of Hindu employés of every kind, inspectors, ticket-sellers, guards, porters, lamplighters, refreshment-sellers, quietly and safely carry on its business. Native booksellers have their shops adorned with the last English romances; piles of newspapers arrive, damp, smelling of printer's ink, great English "papers" of eight pages, loaded with advertisements, stiff, lustrous, and not easily unfolded. Five or six babus came into my waggon, installed by their "boys." They opened the newspapers and lighted their cigarettes. Soft faces, gentle and heavy, English short coats; but their untrousered legs showed brown under the draped muslin of their skirts.

The train moves out: great stores of coal, gasometers, factories, the usual *décor* of the suburbs of a great city. Then the flat country, rice-fields, bouquets of palm-trees, shining in the softest and richest light.

Toward the horizon,—pale blue, but not at all misty,—the sun descends, but without the slightest change of appearance. It melts, yet remains intact, a pure disc of fluid fire, which throbs slowly, sinks insensibly, melts as it touches the plain, vanishes in a rosy light which floats motionless, vaporised upon the horizon's belt, and dies into the blue overhead. There trembles a single star, rayless, like a great drop of perfectly white water. In the zenith the sky grows dark, while the horizon reddens like glowing ashes; and we spin along in the plain, the interminable and empty plain, which now vanishes on all sides into the darkness.

In the north are distinguishable vast pale stretches, vague gleams of light, the distant sheets of water of a great river which has overflowed its banks.

November 25.

In the morning, a vast level country, yellow with grain; then russet with dry grass. This suggests, for some unknown reason, Turguenieff and the Russian steppes. All things awake, in calm of the first hour: the clear cry of large birds which are passing in triangles; in the tall grass, files of men are going to their daily labour. The familiar feeling recurs, to which our own plains give rise—one loves this rich and gentle earth, full of tranquil strength—good to men, to animals, plants, to all existences that quietly pursue their regular life upon its deep breast.

About eight o'clock, straight in front of us, in the open sky, well above the plain, something floated, at which I looked for a long time without thinking about it,—a pale outline, whose paleness and precision finally excite attention. Suddenly comes the thought that this must be the Himalaya, a hundred miles away. So high, so light, its snows, scarcely tinged with blue, seem regions of a thinner air in the dense azure. This cannot possibly be part of the earth. Under it there is nothing; there are no mountains to be seen; there is, again, the void, blue depth of space; and it seems as if this were heaven opened, an inaccessible paradise hung in ether, an abode of the luminous, sovereign *devas*.

At Siliguri we change trains. The first slopes are now only twenty miles away; the approach of a new world makes itself distinctly felt. Beside the slender Bengalis, there are Mongol mountaineers, short and thick-set, with square face, yellow skin, oblique eyes, felt boots, a three-bladed poignard stuck into the belt; and their cloaks of a dark woollen stuff contrast with the light-coloured robes of the effeminate-looking Hindus. This is the frontier of the two races, the limit of two human continents; for the Tartars, who begin here, cover Central Asia and China, extending to the Arctic snows. What an astonishing human variety in this station here, at the foot of the Himalaya! A dozen English officers and planters, two or three German and Swedish travellers, then a crowd of Hindus, Lepchas, Bhutiás. European coats, the white skirts of the Bengalis, the red robes of the Lepcha women,

—who, in feature, ornaments, and dress are almost Siberian,—cloaks from Tibet, are piled into open cars which resemble sledges; the little locomotive whistles, and we run toward the blue wall which bounds the plain.

When the vapours which are pumped up from the ocean by the equatorial sun are driven by the south-west monsoon, they rise into the Indian sky, traversing it in great white multitudes, or melting away in the hot air. In the north they encounter an icy barrier, twenty-three thousand feet high, and they fall in snow or rain upon its slopes. Almost nothing goes beyond. The plateaus of Tibet are arid, the southern slopes receiving all the water drawn from the Indian seas. Nothing can give an idea of these rains. While in London there is an average fall of two feet of water annually, the average here is thirty-one feet. In the year 1861 there was a rainfall of sixty-seven feet. There is great depth of earth, an extreme heat of the sun, and it may be imagined what the vegetation must be. These mountains, whence descend all the great rivers of the plain, spread life throughout Hindustan, and at its source this life has its greatest violence.

Imagine, then, a monstrous elevation, the great backbone of the earth, against which tempests from the ocean break in storms and downpours of water, like the primitive cataclysms of the world; a virgin growth, springing up in this fire and water and mist, where all the trees and all the plants of the world, from jungles of bananas and tropical climbing plants, to forests of fir-trees, are superposed;

add to this the tumult of cataracts, the impetuous cry of the young rivers ; lower down, the mewing of tigers ; high up above the rocks the scream of eagles in the icy air ; everywhere, re-echoing peals of thunder : a dense, violent, noisy life, which seems to stream down from above ; or rather we might say, which ascends into space, becoming fainter, like the murmur of a distant multitude, and expiring in the silent indifference of ice-masses, which project into empty space : and one perhaps will feel the grandeur of this mountain world.

We begin to penetrate it, entering the jungle, the thick fur of trees and plants which extends as far as the snows. Even the Cinhalese forests were not like this : the palms and bamboos, of too rapid growth, seemed fragile there, and the admirable lustre of the stems and leaves was due to a perpetual miracle of heat and light. Here, it is the tree itself, solid, ligneous, ancient, not slender and smooth, but rugged, enormous of trunk. Magnolias, mahogany trees, are buried under heavy green mosses, which from every branch hang like dripping hair. Climbing plants, two hundred feet long, cross from tree to tree, strained like cables, like great snakes stiffened in some effort ; and beneath the lofty forest there is another, a light mist of ferns, thickets of tall plants, of rhododendrons, smothered in the darkness.

Now the first slopes are below us, whence the forests descend, stretching out into the plain, like a great dark cloak fallen at the mountain's feet, spreading itself out in vast folds, in heaps of shining verdure, veiled in luminous vapours, pierced with deep holes of shadow. On one side the mountain opens in an amphitheatre, ten miles broad, full of a thick bluish atmosphere that is visible. Within it, three forests seem to have fallen in, and lie heaped up and reeking in the sunlight, giving out sheets of quivering, resinous heat, exhaling the breath of their mighty vegetable existence.

Beyond, the plains of Bengal extend, vague, indistinct ; they rise toward the sky, vanish, disappear high up in the light and the mist.

At seven thousand feet it is very cold ; we already have the cold of Central Asia. We encounter the fog coming toward us like a vast, grey tide : it moves slowly around the trunks of the great forest, clings to them, invades the thickets, is torn, floats in fragments, reunites, puts out the sun, leaving it a greenish disc like some strange moon. On each side are pale phantoms of giant trees, vaporous glimpses of dripping undergrowth, a foggy, colossal vegetation which seems to have grown up without sunlight, in some world of dreams. How far away we now are from the luminous plain where man languishes in his white muslins ! From time to time appear miserable Lepcha villages, half visible in the wet darkness, little conical huts, almost Chinese, in which blaze huge bright fires ; low, dark shops, full of bananas and oranges from the plain, and smoked meat. A Mongol population, splashing about in the mud ; children like grotesque figures in yellow wax ; little, angular women clad in heavy red woollen garments ; men wrapped in their goat-skin cloaks, with green boots, and little three-peaked felt hats, much more unlike ourselves, with their heavy faces, their projecting cheek-bones, their oblique eyes; much more foreign than the Hindu or the Cinhalese, and telling of an entirely distinct human race. Everything here is Mongol. The yataghans, the objects of lacquered wood, the stunted statuettes that are sold in the largest village, suggest China; it is the same outlandish art, the same curious unshapeliness. How explain this, except by an affinity of race, stronger than barriers and distances, for Tibet is still far away, the other side of the high icy passes, almost inaccessible; and English India is close by!

Suddenly the fog breaks; it flies beneath us, cleft like a torn curtain, and there is revealed in full light, from base to summit, the whole great white chain. We have just reached the crest of the only line of foot-hills which separates the high peaks from the plains of India. Between us and the snows there is only a sombre circular valley of a hundred square leagues, in which the fog adds its darkness to the shadow of the primeval forests. Across the valley, deployed upon an arc of a hundred and fifty degrees, twenty peaks rise to a height of twenty-three thousand feet; they rise out of the depths of the valley like huge waves, stiffened, made solid, in their upward spring. In the centre, opposite us, so near that apparently its fall would reach us where we stand, Kunchain-Junga unrolls the dense jungles of its vast base, lifts its rocky masses, its bluish glaciers, and outlines up there against the cold pallor of the sky the sharp peak of its summit, at a height of twenty-six thousand feet. With a glance the eye measures this prodigious height.

This is what I have before my eyes : in the foreground, along the ridge which we have just reached, specking with white dots the black background of its forests, the little villas of Darjiling, the ultimate verge of the civilised world, on the edge of the abyss of savage Asia, the great unknown country, peopled by yellow races ; then, the dark void of the immense valley, a shadowy amphitheatre filled with shapeless, floating clouds. Five slender, misty rays of light traverse it, reflected from a dazzling mass which is behind us, upon the black shoulder of the mountain. Fixed above the sombre darkness of the floating vapours, these rays measure the gulf. Neither ocean nor desert could give the vertiginous sensation of space, as do these five rigid lines, flung across this valley, forty miles in breadth, closed by a wall twenty-four thousand feet high. In this deep, a confusion of ridges and slopes ; but, above, calm, uplifting, sovereign light, the inviolable serenity of the great summit where unite all the obscure mountain chains, which, in Nepaul, in Tibet, in India, have lifted themselves, and struggled through the darkness to meet each other, and with joint impulse rise above all things into the silence of bright space, and dominate the world.

November 26.

One arrives, prepared by this journey for great emotions ; and here is an English summer resort.

On the road from the station, opposite the Himalaya, are large posters : Colman's Mustard, Pears' Soap, Beecham's Pills; then, a crowd of children on horseback, active, chubby little Saxons, young girls sitting straight in the saddle, the complexion clear, a pink flush on the cheek, wearing jockey caps and perfectly-fitting habits, followed by the Hindu servant, humble in the presence of the stronger race. You pass cottages whose bay-windows are framed in clematis and climbing roses. On the gates of the little gardens are names of English villas, "Birchwood," or "Woodland House." The highest points of Darjiling—whence one's eyes rest upon the entire Sikkim—is dotted with gay little villas, among them rising a little Saxon church tower of grey stone, like those that keep watch over the pale English landscape. Near by, a tennis ground, from which the players, in their flannels, are just going off.

At sight of all this the mind changes its orientation, and old recollections emerge from the darkness in which they slept, old currents of ideas and emotions recur. You are in England, it is sunset of a summer's day, and if you look up, you expect to see the red streaks of the sky across a wan field. Here are the "Assembly Rooms," where there is dancing in the evening, and the first flirtations which lead to marriage. Here is the Dissenting Chapel, which Methodists, Baptists, and Wesleyans enjoy in turn. Here are the scarlet soldiers, athletic, with lustrous hair, who live like gentlemen in their barracks, and, switch in hand, assume airs of importance in the street. Here is the genteel and respectable "boarding-house," such as you may have known at Eastbourne or Scarborough. You put on a black coat for dinner; the mistress of the house says grace, and ceremoniously sends round thin slices of lamb or beef, and heavy bits of "pudding." The husband, a personage of less importance, but correct, adds to the respectability of the house. There is conversation, the tranquil conversation of well-bred people who are not suspicious of one another. In the drawing-room, after dinner, a young lady will seat herself at the piano, and the evening passes with songs from Gilbert and Sullivan's last operetta, or some patriotic or sentimental melody, and there are plans for the next day's excursion.

Compare with this the French colony in Tunis or Tonkin, usually all bachelors! How a man is bored there! How he feels his exile! But these English are in England, here. They have brought hither not only their institutions, their customs, their prejudices, but their whole natural environment, and the *mise en scène* to which they are accustomed. The contact of a different world seems not to affect them at all. In fact, no race is less capable of adaptation, less flexible; none so continuously persists in its own type and personality. Hence, their moral energy, and the force of their will, directed by certain immutable ideas; hence, also, their limited sympathy and comprehension. These people ignore the native entirely, and make no effort to understand him. From the height of their civilisation they regard him as a half-savage "idolater." "Idolater" is the term by which are designated indiscriminately the Hindu, the Buddhist, and the Parsi.* This is quite the Biblical point of view; thus the Jews spoke of other nations. At Ceylon, a planter, who had been resident in the island for fifteen years, put this question to me: "And what are the names of their idols? What is it that they worship?"

Just now I was admiring the *hauteur*, the phlegm, the disdainful silence of two English soldiers in the shop of a vendor of Chinese things; they turned over his bibelots without a glance at himself. This evening, at *table d'hôte*, a young officer, lately arrived, having visited during the day a lama's temple, sums up his impressions briefly: "A nasty hole, which I was only too glad to get out of." The inhabitant is to them only a coolie, "a boy," useful for carrying luggage or blacking boots; as the country to them is only a place for industrial or agricultural exploitation. They cut away the finest forests of Darjiling or of Ceylon that they may cover the denuded soil with their melancholy tea plantations. Make the ascent of the Sinchul, the adjacent height which overlooks Darjiling, and you will see the grandest panorama in the world: southward, the plains of India; on the north, the Himalayan peaks; but the foreground of the picture is pure English —gardens, plantations, villas, churches, barracks.

* In Italy, Germany, and France an Englishman speaks of the inhabitants as "the natives." In English, the word "foreigner" has the same meaning that "barbarian" had among the Greeks.

They *civilise*, and this not only for their own advantage, but from a sense of duty toward the native population. To cover India with railways, to enlarge and multiply its seaports, to increase tenfold its commerce, to convert it to Protestant Christianity, to suppress its castes, to enfranchise its women, to open its *zenanas*, to give it—with a liking for trousers, black coats, cricket, football, English music and poetry—"a practical and sensible education:" in this, say the English, consists their mission in India, being persuaded, with Addison, with Sydney Smith, with Macaulay, that the augmentation of human well-being, a decent, reasonable, comfortable civilisation, in a word, English civilisation, is the chief end and aim of humanity. "When we have finished our work in India," an Englishman said to me in Ceylon, "very probably the Hindus will be able to do without us, and will turn us out. But we shall have accomplished our mission." Thereupon he extolled "the railway which strikes through the forests, brings life and light to the interior of the country, and makes war on old superstitions and Buddhist mummeries." They are so enterprising that India — now furnished with manufactories, railways, universities, banks — has to-day the budget and the commerce of Italy or Austria ; they are so rigid and so strong, that this handful of men among the two hundred million Hindus remain absolutely unchanged, while the Hindu seems to become English from contact with the hundred thousand colonists. At Calcutta I had the opportunity to see books and newspapers of

Hindu authorship; not only was their English excellent, but there were the turns of thought, the style, the prejudices, all the English forms of feeling and thinking. Some articles might have come from the pen of the reverend editor of a well-known magazine published in London. Thus, certain artistic individuals of plastic soul, after talking long with a man of original and powerful personality, unconsciously copy his attitudes and gestures, and the inflections of his voice. "A race of flint," says Carlyle of the Anglo-Saxons: yes, a race of flint, which, imprinting itself without itself suffering abrasion into the soft Hindu clay, stamps all its own angles and projections there. Haughty conquerors, untiring organisers, they are here the noble race, a new Brahman race, *devas* of superior order. And I felt it this morning, when I saw above the grotesque crowd of wretched Mongols, the upright carriage, the calm movement, the tranquil, strong gesture, the bright faces, the serene and determined look of three young Englishmen.

November 27.

I rise before four o'clock to see the first rays of the sun on Kunchain-Junga. It is frosty and dark: nothing is visible but the outlines of neighbouring trees, and, up there among the cold constellations, the waning moon, too slender a crescent to throw any light. There is nothing to be seen, but you know that in every direction the ground steals away, sinks, and you are conscious of the immense dark forests below, and of the country of Sikkim,

THE HIMALAYA DARJILING 69

extending in the darkness. The great chain has disappeared entirely.

About half-past four, high up in| the sky appears a star, a very singular star, for, as you watch it, it seems to grow larger. A spot of rose colour comes, remains, increases. Then sharp outlines are lighted up. Below, the very blackness of night, not a sign of dawn, the earth asleep in the darkness; and you are afraid of those luminous things appearing up there in space, that light not of this world, which seems a prelude to some stupendous change in the established order.

Then all the snowy summits, coming out of the night, are lighted up like the mysterious shore of a pink sea; and then, a long time after, the old forests reappear.

About seven o'clock I took a guide to penetrate a little the mystery of the jungle. We follow a route lying along the edge of the great valley and commanding it. Below us, out of the dense thickets, tree-ferns arise, like palms, out of their sheath of tawny moss soaked in dew. Farther down, the jungle descends, with its domes of lustrous trees, seen from above, half veiled by the heavy air—descends to the bottom of the great valley of the Sikkim, which, four thousand feet below the road, displays the sombre stretch of its virgin forests. Beyond, above the bluish vegetation, begin the glacier-streaks, and high white outlines cut sharply the pale sky.

My guide walks with a strong, heavy step, the step of the mountaineers of Tibet—a true Chinese type; not the delicate, slender Chinese, but the man of the North, tall and angular. A face ploughed by deep wrinkles, chapped, tanned by the sun. A small, green, three-peaked hat, whence descends a black queue of braided hair, an immense sheep-skin cloak, boots of green felt turned up in very long points. Savage ornaments : a green ring, and another of ivory on the thumb; the left ear stretched, lengthened by a silver disc. He walks on silently, with his regular step, leaning on a great teak-wood pike, covered with pointed characters that are unlike the Hindustani letters, complicated with a sundial whereby the Tibetans read the hour, when they roam their vast desert-plateau beyond the Himalaya. Sometimes, with a motion of the arm, a slow smile, and gutturals which are not human, he designates the remote mountains. We communicate by signs—he, the strange Mongolian man, whose race, since the first days of humanity, has roamed the steppes of Central Asia; I, the Parisian tourist, arriving in this land after the long voyage over monotonous seas. What an abyss between his race and mine ! Impossible to find for us a common origin, in the darkness of the past ! Impossible to understand this motionless face, shut against me, this face not made like ours, in which the soul cannot be read.

On the edge of the road, as I examined with surprise a rock curiously carved, he twice raised his arm toward heaven, toward the sun, I think. This time he seems to have understood me. The same gesture, before a row of long poles whence hang white rags covered with sacred characters. These poor banners are religious emblems, and have innumerable prayers inscribed upon them. A wind blows them toward the sky, and all these silent prayers are heard. At this moment they hang inert, along a narrow pathway which goes down to the miserable hovels of a community of lamas, on the side of the great valley. At its entrance a lad, a novice, seated on the ground, is reciting, with nasal tone, prayers written in Chinese on old strips of some woven fabric. Emerges, from a corner where he had crouched invisible, a yellowish creature, a lama, who comes up and walks around us, making profound salutations, his hands lifted to his forehead. He is horrible and pitiable, this lama, really unnatural; all the Tartar traits exaggerated, the eyes bloodshot, no chin at all, the mouth lost in the flabby fold of the yellowish neck, the expression brutish and rigid.

At the door a row of prayer cylinders, which my guide has had an eye on for some minutes. Furtively he goes up to them, and, with an enigmatical smile, one by one, without haste, he turns them all. What is he thinking of, while in a low voice he mutters his gutturals? What is the obscure emotion which has dictated his act?

In the interior, behind a glass case, the vague sketch of a seated Buddha, not calm and smiling, but grimacing with a Mongol grimace. Before him on an altar, offerings—poor offerings, not sumptuous flowers, as in Ceylon, but grains of rice, some water, and, in old English gin or whisky bottles, some miserable withered plants. All this tells of a primitive and barbaric poverty. On the walls, very ancient frescos are scaling off, ancient bluish paintings which seem to have been monsters of the Mongol imagination, hideous to see. "Darjiling," says the lama, indicating one of them; another is Kunchain-Junga, the mountain. By what mysterious association of ideas has that grand, simple, noble form a shapeless, complicated dragon for its symbol? What kind of vague emotion, terror, or sadness, did the view awaken in their ancestors?

I slip a few annas into the yellow paw which the poor lama slyly extends to me, and we leave the little mud temple, in the shadow of its floating banners, under the guard of the thousand prayers which stream in the wind, clinging all solitary on the edge of the great misty amphitheatre.

This evening, all the space is filled with clouds, and grey vapours drown the valleys which go toward India or toward China. Far away in the west there are gleams of rose-colour, of unknown origin. Upon the black sides of the mountains and on the crowded peaks there is a slow, monotonous procession of grey things, creeping upward interminably. In this pale mist the lower spurs of the mountains, crossing each other, are distinguishable only as superposed walls of blackness. And this produces a vague infinitude, not of surface, like the ocean, but of depth, wherein is outlined a dark world where slowly gather incompleted shapes, spaces of shadow, confused lights, conjectural forests, ridges that cross each other, blue rays darting across the void : a grey, undulating confusion.

Upon a ridge one tall twisted tree seems to mark the world's end, on the edge of the abyss. Below, nothing : a vaporous chaos, wherein vague forms are floating. Literally, one seems to have come to empty space, to the world's misty edge, and only chaos beyond.

At this moment I hear singing,—clear childish voices from a school of little English girls, which is somewhere here on the hill ; it is like a memory of childhood coming to a man at the last instant of his life, with the darkness of the Beyond before him. What is it that fills these moments with so painful and subtle emotion ? why are these sunsets so mysteriously sad, impressing themselves more deeply upon the memory than all the grand sights one has come so far to see ?

The tree shivers in all its branches, and the grey vapour creeps higher and higher upon the wan background of the sky. And now, the Sikkim is buried in fog. But above all this melancholy confusion, one remembers that the great crimsoned summits rise, that they rest upon a bed of quiet cloud, alone in the presence of the dying sun.

CHAPTER V

BENARES   BRAHMANISM   HINDUISM

November 29.

A SUDDEN scene-shifting. Yesterday evening I arrived here after twenty-four hours on the Bengal Northern, and twenty-one hours on the Great Peninsular. On the road there is nothing to see. From the cold Mongol regions we come down at once into the sacred plains of India, through which flows the ancient, divine Ganges.

For this is classic India, India of the Indians. Here, the European has no dwelling-place ; he only passes through. He has transformed nothing, has established himself neither as merchant nor manufacturer. This city, these Hindus, these temples are the same to-day that they were ten centuries ago. This is the heart of the Hindu world, the very focus of Brahmanism. Those old Brahmans who, "after they have seen the sons of their sons," go away into the depths of the forest, there to remain in solitary meditation on the substance of things, go from Benares or from adjacent parts of the Ganges valley. Upon this soil were elaborated the six great systems of Hindu philosophy. Twenty-five centuries ago this city was already famous. Yes, when Babylon was struggling with Nineveh ; when

Tyre was throwing out her colonies along the shores of the Mediterranean; before the *agora* of Athens resounded with the eloquence of her orators, and the temples of Greece were peopled with their marble statues; when Rome was but a peasant hamlet; when the old Egyptian cults were in their prime; then, this city, great and famous, was filled, as it is to-day, with white-skinned Brahmans, in feature resembling those of to-day, even then bowed down by a ritualistic tyranny, crushed in upon themselves, absorbed in metaphysical speculations, indefinitely dividing the fine-spun thread, arriving at vertigo, and in their hallucination seeing the solid earth give way and sink into that calm nothingness whence eternally arise the appearances of things. Sakya-Muni was one of these Brahmans; he was born not a hundred miles from here, and, after his five years' meditation, he came to preach at Benares.

To-day not a trace remains of our European world as it then was; it is altogether dead, finished, buried in the abyss of time. But this city of Benares remains always the Kasi, "the resplendent city," of India.

In the morning, when the throbbing disc of the sun rises behind the Ganges, twenty-five thousand Brahmans, crouching on the river bank, in the presence of the Hindu multitude, repeat the old Vedic hymns to the sun, to the divine river, the primitive powers, the visible sources of life. Rome is not so sacred to the Catholic as is Benares to the Hindu; each stone of it is holy. No pollution, no sin can endanger the man who dies within its walls. Were he Christian, were he Musalman, had he even killed a cow or eaten its flesh, he is no less certainly transported into the Kailasa, the Himalayan paradise of Siva. Happy, therefore, the man who can die within the walls of Benares! More than two hundred thousand pilgrims come hither every year from all parts of India; among them, many old men and many incurably ill. When a man could not come here to die, often his ashes are brought, that "the sons of the Ganges," the Brahmans of Benares, may pronounce the prayers of the dead, and the sacred river may accept them. "Kasi, holy Kasi," say the Hindus; "a man dies peacefully when he has seen thee!"

This city is most extraordinary: elsewhere religion is only part of the public life; at Benares there is nothing else to be seen. It fills everything, occupying every moment of man's existence, and covering the city with its temples. There are more than nineteen hundred of them; and the multitude of chapels is past all counting. As to the idol population, it is nearly twice as numerous as the human, something like five hundred thousand.

Yesterday evening, on arriving, as it was still daylight, I walked as far as the river. The tortuous lanes swarm with half-naked humanity. At the entrance to the sacred places, the crowd is more dense: white-faced Brahmans jostle and elbow you; fakirs sitting on their heels, naked, covered with ashes, the bald head lustrous, the eye fixed, thus motionless in the universal swarming, seem made of stone. Stalls overflow with religious objects, necklaces of yellow flowers, rosaries, sacred stones, strange emblems. In the walls, above the doors, niches shelter shapeless divinities, monstrous gods with heads of elephants and bodies encircled with serpents. Here and there, wells, from which ascends a fetid odour of decayed flowers, are inhabited by gods, and around them the crowd is dense. Upon the walls blue paintings narrate the Hindu mythology; the temples are girt with a garland of obscene divinities, and in the midst of the streets, as if the temples were not numerous enough to contain all the idols, small altars make a pedestal for the fat Ganesa or the shapeless Kali. One's foot slips in the heaps of decaying flowers, there is a strange mud of ordures and sacred jasmine putrefying in this Ganges water with which all the altars are sprinkled; and from the glutinous soil rises a strange, nauseating odour. In the midst of the human multitude monkeys gambol and chatter, clinging to the roofs, and cows wander freely and eat the flowers. And you have the same sensation of bewilderment and vertigo as in reading the old Hindu poems, which make the mind faint with their accumulation of myriads of millions of ages, with their endless enumeration of gods and elements and plants and animals, whirling and intertwined. All our mental habits are set at naught. Imagine yourself to have landed in a country where the inhabitants walk on their heads. This race thinks, and feels, and lives in a fashion contrary to our own; and one's first idea on arriving in Benares is that insanity is normal here.

November 30.

I rise at five. At half-past six I am on the river. Fresh morning light, white in the horizon as liquid silver. The broad Ganges spreads its brown surface, rolling its muddy, choppy current between desert stretches of sand on the left bank and on the right a league of temples, palaces, mosques, marble walls, whose long line disappears in a rosy mist. Immense stairs descend in a grand sweep to the water's edge, and their parallel lines make a broad oblique surface, all glittering in the sunshine. In this light swarm the Hindu people—pilgrims, worshippers, priests, who come to perform their matutinal devotions, to adore the Ganges and the rising sun. They are there by thousands, fat, white old Brahmans, seated on stone tables, a huge straw umbrella over their heads, reading the sacred texts to the crowd who are dabbling in the water; brown *Sudras*, with heads shaven except for a little tuft falling backward, supple in their dark nudity; women, draped from head to foot in brilliant colour, who pray standing, with arms lifted and clasped hands stretched toward the sun. As my boat advances over the shining water, the temples and the crowd are more numerous. Flights of steps, four hundred feet broad, rise in enormous pyramids, striped with their thousand stairs. Massive octagonal pillars plunge into the water; square façades, great carved cones of red stone, cubes of marble whose sides are excavated into niches, chapels, succeed each other, or are piled one behind another : it is a colossal accumulation of stone, lavished, superposed, in geometrical constructions, as in ancient Egypt or in the legendary Assyrian cities. And under all this architecture, on the bank of the old river, a hundred thousand Hindus are in motion, fulfilling their religious rites.

For four hours I go up and down on the river. How describe this inexhaustible variety, this endless succession of forms and attitudes ? Upon the broad steps white in the sunlight, between the piles,—higher up, upon the terraces and upon the heaped blocks of ruined temples,—still higher upon balconies and roofs of massive stone, under a forest of straw parasols, the same swarming of brown figures, the same flutter of simple colours. Five nude figures, crouching upon a pillar, abruptly separate, flinging themselves into the water, which splashes up in every direction. Behind these, Brahmans, with lips moving in prayer, are waving branches and monotonously strike the water with them. Below, women emerge from the river, serious and upright in their dripping blue mantles which cling closely, moulding the figure. Crouching on a high marble block, isolated from the crowd, a man wrapped in red silk, motionless, in a hieratic posture regards the sun. Then, strange attitudes and gestures as of maniacs : two women grasping the nose with one hand, and with the other striking the breast; a trembling old woman, her poor body outlined in all its meagreness by the dripping garment, joining her wrinkled hands and whirling six times consecutively. Others, with a rapid vibration of the lips, splash the water methodically, making it spurt away from them; old men in attitudes of river-gods, hold copper vases. And, as background to all this, behind the countless conical chapels on the stairs themselves, a row of eighty temples and palaces. I notice one larger than the rest, a vast rose-coloured cube, sharply relieved against the sky, flowery with balconies, covered with arabesques, notched with colonnettes, pierced by its windows with arched shadows. It flings down to the water's edge its grand staircase, which stretches a broad oblique sheet of glittering white; and upon its highest steps, nude men are straining their lustrous muscles, brandishing clubs, designing heroic silhouettes upon the marble.

We have gone over two miles, and the spectacle is the same. The crowd, the architecture, the sunlight, seem to be visions of some opium-dream, where time, space, and all that they contain, appear enormously magnified and multiplied. Here, as farther down the river, at the foot of the edifices are platforms of wood or stone, making out into the luminous water, and each has its own swarm, a hundred women draped in white, bending over the water; figures of young men, standing erect; Brahmans, motionless, meagre, with salient vertebræ, bent over, as absorbed in some doleful reverie; groups of children gambolling around funeral piles, on which the dead are burned; sacred cows, in quiet outlines against the white of the marble stairs; and from all this moving, praying, singing multitude rises a great noise, a confused rustle of human life. Everywhere on the edge of the great careless river there is the same swarming life, the same vast wave of humanity heaping itself up.

Thousands of pigeons fly about and light upon cones of temples; grey crows and great vultures with pendent crops pose upon bases of columns. The air is noisy with the chatter of magnificent parrots; smoke ascends from the cremation of dead bodies, and here and there the river is black with ashes that have been thrown into it. Great patches of flowers are floating down the current; prayers without number are ascending to Siva, to Durga, to Ganesa, to Surya, the sun, which has become burning. In presence of the great river, among the pyramids of stone, under the colonnades of the chapels, at the foot of these huge edifices—strange as Indian vegetation and Indian religion—swarms the infinite life of India. For a moment you seem to feel, in yourself, the overwhelming sensation which, repeated for generations, modifying the structure of the Aryan brain, has translated itself into their poems and their philosophies.

Behind individual and perishable existences you feel the force which unfolds itself to produce all things and all lives, imperishable, eternally present, always the same, amid the millions of deaths and

F

births which manifest, but do not diminish it. It is this force which they adore; it is the cult of this force which is the substance of their religion. When once this is understood and felt, it becomes possible to understand the contradictions, the incoherences, of this complex Hinduism, where a fetichism as of savages is allied to the profoundest speculation ; which adores three hundred and thirty million gods, and also animals, trees, elements, plants, stones ; at once pantheistic, polytheistic, and monotheistic, according to its method of regarding the Universal Being, his principal incarnation, certain portions, or the totality of his manifestations in matter or in spirit. This being once understood, it explains the insanities of their imagination, the strangeness of their dreams, which find expression in those interminable, bushy poems, where man, overwhelmed by nature, has for equals and comrades the monkey, the bear, elephants, plants, insects. In them all there is life, coming and going in waves, dying and being born, multifold, infinitely diverse. And the contrast made it all more clear to me when I saw, above this confused multitude, above this inflorescence of temples, springing up white against the blue of the sky the two minarets of a Musalman mosque. They sprang straight upward, with the ardour of a prayer, with the impetuosity of a cry ; and one perceived the fervent work of a simple, resolute, monotheistic, and ardent race.

Noon. I leave the river, and am driven rapidly through the city. Very quickly the lanes, the shops, the chased copper spread out on the sidewalks, the temples, the idols in the streets, fly past us. Then, the dusty country. At the hotel it is a strange sensation to come back to European tranquillity and reasonableness, fine, calm order, correct costume, commonplace and courteous conversation. You fall back into your accustomed place, and the impression of what you have just seen disappears like a dream. And still, a certain disturbance remains. If we see a man who makes frantic gestures, talks incoherently, conducts himself differently from the rest of us in all respects, we have no hesitation in saying he acts like a madman. But when you have been alone in the midst of an entire population who are acting thus, you need to be very strong and sure of yourself to express such an opinion. Here, myself and my neighbour at the *table d'hôte* are the exceptions. You doubt, at least, if there *is* a rule, or an exception; you lose your bearings; you have no longer a standard by which you measure things and are accustomed to see others measure them. It impresses you strongly that our European ideas and customs are only local ideas and customs; that our point of view is merely *different* from the Hindu point of view; that, in substance, one is as valid as the other; and that all fashions of existence are legitimate, in that they exist. By what right have I said that the normal condition of this people is insanity?

After tiffin I hesitate in deciding what to do; outdoors the sun blazes down upon a country which at this hour is entirely deserted. I open certain books, that I may seek the meaning of what I have seen. What do these rites signify, these gestures as of maniacs—what do they indicate? After an hour's reading the primitive sensation recurs: these men certainly must be mad.

Here is the daily life of one of the twenty-five thousand Brahmans of Benares. He rises before the dawn, and his first care is to look at an object of good omen. If he sees a crow at his left, a kite, a snake, a cat, a hare, a jackal, an empty jar, a smoking fire, a wood-pile, a widow, a man blind of one eye, he is threatened with great dangers during the day; if he intended to make a journey, he puts it off. But if he sees a cow, a horse, an elephant, a parrot, a lizard, a clear-burning fire, a virgin, all will go well. If he should sneeze once, he may count upon some special good fortune; but if twice, some disaster will happen to him. If he yawns, some demon may enter his body. Having avoided all objects of evil omen, the Brahman drops into the endless routine of his religious rites. Under penalty of rendering all the day's acts worthless, he must wash his teeth at the bank of a sacred stream or lake, reciting a special *mantra*, which ends in this ascription:

"O Ganges, daughter of Vishnu, thou springest from Vishnu's foot, thou art beloved by him! Remove from us the stains of sin and of birth; and, until death, protect us, thy servants!"

He then rubs his body with ashes, saying: "Homage to Siva, homage to the source of all birth! May he protect me during all births!" He traces the sacred signs upon his forehead—the three vertical lines representing the foot of Vishnu, or the three horizontal lines which symbolise the trident of Siva, and twists into a knot the hair left by the razor on the top of his head, that no impurity may fall from it to pollute the sacred river.

He is now ready to begin the ceremonies of the morning (*sandhya*), those which I have just observed on the banks of the river. Minutely and mechanically each Brahman performs by himself these rites of prescribed acts and gestures.

First, the internal ablution: the worshipper takes water in the hollow of his hand, and, letting it fall from above into his mouth, cleanses his body and soul. Meanwhile he mentally invokes the twenty-four names of Vishnu, saying: "Glory to Kesava, to Narayana, to Madhava, to Govinda," and so on.

The second rite is the exercise or "discipline" of the respiration (*prajayama*). Here there are three acts: first, the worshipper compresses the right nostril with the thumb, and drives the breath through the left; second, he inhales through the left nostril, then compresses it, and inhales through the other; third, he stops the nose completely with thumb and forefinger, and holds his breath as long as possible.

All these acts must be done before sunrise, and prepare for what is to follow. Standing on the water's edge, he utters solemnly the famous syllable OM, pronouncing it *aum*, with a length equalling that of three letters. It recalls to him the three persons of the Hindu trinity : Brahma, who creates ; Vishnu, who preserves ; Siva, who destroys. More noble than any other word, imperishable, says Manu, it is eternal as Brahma himself. It is not a sign, but a being, a force ; a force which constrains the gods, superior to them, the very essence of all things. Mysterious operations of the mind, strange associations of ideas, from which spring conceptions like these !

Having uttered this ancient and formidable syllable, the man calls by their names the three worlds : earth, air, sky ; and the four superior heavens. He then turns toward the east, and repeats the verse from the Rig-Veda : "Let us meditate upon the resplendent glory of the divine vivifier, that it may enlighten our minds." As he says the last words he takes water in the palm of his hand and pours it upon the top of his head. "Waters," he says, "give me strength and vigour that I may rejoice. Like loving mothers, bless us, penetrate us with your sacred essence. We come to wash ourselves from the pollution of sins : make us fruitful and prosperous." Then follow other ablutions, other *mantras*, verses from the Rig-Veda, and this hymn, which relates the origin of all things : "From the burning heat came out all beings. Yes, the complete order of the world : Night, the throbbing Ocean, and after the throbbing Ocean, Time, which separates Light from Darkness. All mortals are its subjects. It is this which disposes of all things, and has made, one after another, the sun, the moon, the sky, the earth, the intermediate air." This hymn, says Manu, thrice repeated, effaces the gravest sins.

About this time, beyond the sands of the opposite shore of the Ganges, the sun appears. As soon as its brilliant disc becomes visible the multitude welcome it, and salute it with "the offering of water." This is thrown into the air, either from a vase or from the hand. Thrice the worshipper, standing in the river up to his waist, flings the water toward the sun. The farther and wider he flings it, the greater the virtue attributed to this act. Then the Brahman, seated upon his heels, fulfils the most sacred of his religious duties : he meditates upon his fingers. For the fingers are sacred, inhabited by different manifestations of Vishnu : the thumb by Govinda, the index finger by Mahidhava, the middle finger by Hrikesa, the third by Trivikama, the little finger by Vishnu himself, while Madhava resides in the thumb. "Homage to the two thumbs," says the Brahman, ": to the two index fingers, to the two middle fingers, to the two 'unnamed fingers,' to the two little fingers, to the two palms, to the two backs of the hand." Then he touches the various parts of his body, and lastly, the right ear, the most sacred of all, where resides fire, water, the sun, and the moon. He then takes a red bag (*gomukhi*), into which he plunges his hand, and by contortions of the fingers rapidly represents the chief incarnations of Vishnu : a fish, a tortoise, a wild boar, a lion, a slip-knot, a garland. There are a hundred and eight of these figures, of which not one should be omitted, and the merits attached to these gestures are infinite.

The second part of the service is no less rich than the first in ablutions and *mantras*. The Brahman invokes the sun, " Mitra, who regards all creatures with unchanging gaze," and the Dawns, "brilliant children of the sky," the earliest divinities of our Aryan races. He extols the world of Brahma, that of Siva, that of Vishnu ; recites passages from the Mahabharata, the Puranas, all the first hymn of the Rig-Veda, the first lines of the second, the first words of the principal Vedas, of the Yajur, the Sama, and the Atharva, then fragments of grammar, inspired prosodies, and, in conclusion, the first words of the book of the Laws of Yajnavalkya, the philosophic Sutras : and finally ends the ceremony with three kinds of ablutions, which are called the refreshing of the gods, of the sages, and of the ancestors.

First placing his sacred cord upon the left shoulder, the Brahman takes up water in the right hand and lets it run off his extended fingers. To refresh the sages, the cord must hang about the neck, and the water run over the side of the hand between the thumb and the fore-finger, which is bent back. For the ancestors, the cord passes over the right shoulder, and the water falls from the hand in the same way as for the sages. "Let the fathers be refreshed," says the prayer ; "may this water serve all those who inhabit the seven worlds, as far as to Brahma's dwelling, even though their number be greater than thousands of millions of families. May this water, consecrated by my cord, be accepted by the men of my race who have left no sons."

With this prayer the morning service ends. Now, remember that this worship is daily, that these formulas must be pronounced, these movements of the hands made, with mechanical precision; that if the worshipper forgets the fiftieth one of the incarnations of Vishnu which he is to figure with his fingers, if he stop his left nostril when it should be the right, the entire ceremony loses its efficacy; that, not to go astray amid this multitude of words and gestures required for each rite, he is obliged to use mnemotechnic methods; that there are five of these for each series of formulas; that his attention always strained and always directed toward the externals of the cult, does not leave his mind a moment in which to reflect upon the profound meaning of some of these prayers; and you will comprehend the extraordinary scene that the banks of the Ganges at Benares present every morning; this anxious and demented multitude, these gestures, eager and yet methodical, this rapid movement of the lips, the fixed gaze of these men and women who, standing in the water, seem not even to see their neighbours, and count mentally like men in the delirium of a fever. Remember that there are ceremonies like these in the afternoon, and also in the evening; and that, in the intervals, in the street, in the house at meals, when going to bed, similar rites no less minute pursue the Brahman, all preceded by the exercises of respiration, the enunciation of the syllable OM, and the invocation of the principal gods. It is estimated that between daybreak and noon he has scarcely an hour of rest from the performance of these rites. After the great powers of nature, the Ganges, the Dawn, and the Sun, he goes to worship, in their temples, the representations of divinity, the sacred trees, finally, the cows, to whom he offers flowers. In his own dwelling other divinities await him : five black stones, representing Siva, Ganesa, Surya, Devi, and Vishnu, arranged according to the cardinal points ; one toward the north, a second to the south-east, a third to the south-west, a fourth to the north-west, and one in the centre, this order changing according as the worshipper regards one god or another as most important ; then there is a shell, a bell—to which, kneeling, he offers flowers —and, lastly, a vase, whose mouth contains Vishnu, the neck Rudra, the paunch Brahma, while at the bottom repose the three divine mothers, the Ganges, the Indus, and the Jumna.

This is the daily cult of the Brahman of Benares, and on holidays it is still further complicated. Since the great epoch of Brahmanism it has remained the same. Some details may alter, but as a whole it has always been thus tyrannical and thus extravagant. As far back as the Upanishads appears the same faith in the power of articulate speech, the same imperative and innumerable prescriptions, the same singular formulas, the same enumeration of grotesque gestures. Every day, for more than twenty-five hundred years, since Buddhism was a protest against the tyranny and absurdity of rites, has this race mechanically passed through this machinery, resulting in what mental malformations, what habitual attitudes of mind and will, the race is now too different from ourselves for us to be able to conceive. A negro, a Tierra del Fuegan savage, resembles us more than do these people. The negro is more simple than we, nearer to the life of the animals; but, if we divest ourselves of the unstable acquirements of our civilisation, we discover, concealed, yet alive, in the depths of our souls nearly all of his instincts. On the contrary, the Hindu soul is as completely developed as our own; its vegetation is no less rich, but it is entirely different. It is stupefying to see the crowd of ideas, according to us incoherent and absurd, that form the substance of their minds. Each man belongs to a caste, in which, like his ancestors, he is inexorably shut up. At bottom, the idea of caste is as the idea of species among animals. The distinction between a dog and a bull is of the same nature as that between a Sudra and a Brahman. Hence the horror attaching to the idea of marriage between persons of different castes. Notice that to-day the castes are as numerous as the trades and professions. Each Hindu is born a priest or a doctor, a scribe or a potter, a blacksmith or an engraver; and he believes himself lost if a man of lower caste touches his food or eats at his side. If he quits India, if he crosses the sea, he becomes a pariah : that is to say, he loses his relatives and friends, and can neither buy nor sell, eat, drink, nor live, with any person whatever. He is polluted, and nothing can efface this pollution but the *supreme purification*, the purification "by the cow." Having given large sums of money to the Brahmans, and called together the men of his caste, he swallows the four products of this most sacred of animals, a paste made of the milk and butter and the solid and liquid excrement of the cow. For this animal is one of the high incarnations of divinity, inferior to the Brahman, but superior to almost all the rest of humanity.

Our Hindu has many gods, strange deities not well suited to give habits of order and perspicacity to the brain that seeks to conceive of them. In substance they are almost all metaphysical beings, so abstract that they escape the grasp of the ordinary mind. For example: Kali is "the energy of Siva," and Siva himself, the eternal power which persists under the change of appearances. These are religious ideas which could not be considered anthropomorphic, scarcely capable even of figured representation. But Kali peoples the temples with her idols. She is a black monster, greedy for blood. Children were formerly sacrificed to her, but now goats are immolated on her altars. No cult is so pleasing to her as the repetition of those of her names which contain the letter M. You think you have grasped her and understand her; but, behold, she is transformed; she melts away, her attributes change, she becomes identified with Durga, with Parvati, with Samunda. She was black and hideous; she is now seductive and beautiful. Her forms are endless: an enchanting girl of sixteen ; a nude, headless woman ; a stork ; a puff of smoke.

In the same way Siva is a giant and a dwarf, he has a blue neck, he is clothed in skins, he is a destructive monster, he is a kindly and amorous divinity ; he has one thousand and eight manifestations and a name for each. At times he is confused with Vishnu ; the man intending to worship Siva, worships Vishnu and his diverse incarnations, the fish, the halter, the wild boar, the string. The Hindu also worships Ganesa, and if he writes a book, dedicates it to him as the god of literature. And how does he conceive of this divinity ? As a fat, white Brahman, whose face ends in an elephant's trunk !

When the Brahman prays, after having held his breath as long as possible, he repeats, up to the sixty-fourth time, the same *mantra*. He believes in the supernatural virtue of simple syllables. "*Am* for the forehead," he says in honour of Durga, "*Im* for the right eye, *Im* for the left eye, *Um* for the right ear, *Um* for the left ear, *Rim* for the right nostril, *Rim* for the left nostril." Not content with his three hundred and thirty million gods, he also reveres animals, plants, and stones. Sacred cows block up the temples, bulls roam freely through the streets. To buy grass and give it to these animals is a meritorious act. The sacred places are zoological gardens, where pigeons fly, where cows low, where monkeys chatter ; and out of this confusion of men and animals arise strange odours and a marvellous uproar. The monkeys have their temple, where no man enters except unshod. A rajah on one occasion solemnly celebrated the marriage of a pair of orang-outangs: a hundred thousand rupees were expended in ceremonies, fêtes, and sacrifices. The male monkey, drawn about the city on a car, attended by an army of worshippers, wore a crown; and the rejoicings lasted two weeks. In the neighbouring city of Allahabad, where snakes are gods, the priests and worshippers creep up to the summit of the hill where the temple stands, with writhings and contortions as of snakes! Peacocks, too, are worshipped, and eagles, tortoises, crows, crocodiles. "Pay respect to dogs," says a hymn, "and to the lords of dogs; to horses, and to the lords of horses."

The same worship is paid to certain trees, certain flowers, to black stones, to round stones, to stones used as flat-irons, to razors, ploughs, bellows, and scissors. It may be affirmed that there is no creature of the animal world, no vegetable or mineral object, which is not divine in some part of India. In the midst of these mad ideas, there are intuitions of broad scope upon the divinity of Nature, on the radical unity underlying all her manifestations. "Venerate," says the Hindu hymn, "venerate and honour the eternal masculine, Perusha, who has thousands of names, thousands of forms, thousands of eyes, thousands of heads, thousands of arms, and lives for ten thousand million years."

Our Hindu has his ethics. An inner voice dictates to him certain actions, which it is meritorious to perform and criminal to neglect. But his code and ours have no similarity whatever. Every society rests upon a certain number of sentiments common to all its members, which check or direct the selfish instincts that would tend to the undue development of the individual at the expense of his neighbours and of the harmonious life of the whole group. It cannot be denied that these sentiments vary; and as they vary, the form and structure, the power, and the cohesive strength of the society, differ. They may be very simple, as in the ancient cities; they may be very complex, as in our modern communities, where, slowly, through the ages, extremely diverse circumstances have superposed upon the ancient instincts a great variety of delicate sentiments. But, simple or complicated, they are a condition without which social life is impossible. With the Hindus ethics have a different origin, it seems, and a different character. They are not a code of duties toward one's neighbour; they are nothing but a series of prescriptions regulating the external life, actions, food, and dress. Imagine that, in the Middle Ages, had disappeared the social instinct which forbade a man to betray, to lie, to steal, to murder, to do violence to women, and also the sense of honour which commanded him to fight bravely, to protect his vassal, to follow his suzerain, to stand by his comrade, to sacrifice himself for the band in which he is enrolled, to keep his plighted word, to be solicitous as to his own reputation. Suppress entirely religious morality, consecrating these sentiments; and retain only the religious observances commanded by the Church, to attend Mass, to communicate at Easter, to confess, fast, observe Lent, have one's children baptized, submit to extreme unction : now multiply these observances infinitely, so that they fill the man's entire life, and you have an idea of the Hindu's moral law.

It is not forbidden him to lie ; it is not forbidden him to steal : before the English rule, certain sects commanded assassination, or honoured Siva by an organised violation of women. But if the Hindu sees meat eaten, if he swallows a cow's hair in a cup of insufficiently filtered milk, he is lost, condemned to the worst transmigrations—to the hells of blood, of boiling oil, of reptiles, of molten copper : more than that, he has a horror of himself, for these commands and these prohibitions are not addressed to the outer man only ; there are sentiments corresponding to them, deep-rooted by an observance of twenty-five centuries — organic, traditional sentiments, which form the very substance of the moral nature, enduring through life, entirely independent of changing circumstances or ideas, real categorical imperatives like those which, with us, forbid murder and theft. Intelligent babus, well informed as to our ideas, our sciences, European in philosophy and ethics, have been seen to faint dead away with horror at having by accident tasted bouillon. In 1857 the Sepoys, having the idea that the cartridges which they must tear with their teeth were greased with animal fat, revolted like men in desperation and mad with terror. Formerly, when the English were careless about observing the caste rules in prisons, men under sentence for murder would let themselves die of hunger rather than touch the polluting food. To disobey a precept of which the origin and the object are alike absolutely unknown is the Hindu idea of *sin*—the abominable and deadly sin. A strange sin, moreover, for which neither repentance nor subsequent right action can make amends; and only to be effaced by the mechanical performance of an entirely meaningless act, the repetition of a syllable, a bath in the Ganges, a plunge into some fetid well inhabited by Siva. To touch a Brahman's ear; to listen to the story of Ganga's descent; to eat, at certain fixed times, a mixture of rice and peas—these are all-powerful means of redemption. Every Hindu knows the edifying story of Ajamil, the assassin saved by Vishnu, because, as he was dying, he called for his son Narayana, and this name designates one of the god's incarnations; or of Valmik, the robber whom Siva carries away to the paradise of Kailasa, because he had often cried out: "Mar! mar!" which means, "Kill! kill!" and this word inverted (*Ram*) is the name of the great Rama!

If we look at certain general customs, they manifest no less clearly the strangeness, the contradictions, in the habitual sentiments of this people. Here on every side, in the streets, are birds living unmolested in the midst of the human crowd; here are blue peacocks, that wander through the city at will. Observe the hospitals for sick animals, where are tenderly cared for all sorts of living creatures, dogs, gazelles, eagles. Is it not a sign of the gentle character, the radical goodness of these Hindus? But in 1857 they outdid in cruelty the aborigines of America; and though public human sacrifices have disappeared under the English rule, there is sometimes seen a child's dead body upon an altar of the hideous Kali. Love is unknown in India. Children are married to each other when they are nine years old, then strictly separated till the age of maturity. After that time, the woman is immured. Except her female relatives, no person sees her; no friend may make allusion to her existence even in the most remote way. If the husband learns that she has seen a kinsman, has spoken even to a brother, he brands her in some way; he may, if he will, cut off her nose. As a widow she becomes a pariah, an object of evil omen, whom all avoid with disgust. The married man is not held to fidelity, or even the merest external decency. Those offences against morality that we surround with so much reserve and secrecy are here paraded in the open day; no religious law requires their concealment. More than this, there is a recognised caste of prostitutes; their trade is a sacred duty; and in the south of India every temple has its troop of bayaderes. A sect of Saktists, worshippers of "the energy of Siva," "the force that develops the world," on their feast-days are even released from all distinctions of castes and ties of relationship. Men and women assume a mystic character; they are no longer individuals, but direct incarnations of Siva and Kali. "All men are myself," says the god to the goddess. After drinking wine and intoxicating liquors, eating fish and meat and rice, the union of Kali and Siva is celebrated with inconceivable orgies, and the worshippers feel the limits of personality disappear; they become absorbed in Siva, identified with "the soul of the world."

This cult is "the path leading to the highest form of salvation"; absorption, that is to say, in the Supreme Existence. He who follows it is called *Siddha*, the perfect one; he who knows it not is a *pasu*, a beast, an impure being. "For," says one of their texts, "there is salvation in the use of intoxicating liquors and animal food, and in union with women." It is true this is only a sect among the Hindus; but the point to be noted is that these ideas, which to us appear inconceivable and incredible, dwell familiarly in their minds; that the Hindu does not possess those fundamental sentiments and ideas which, with us, would oppose to notions like these an insurmountable barrier and throw them outside the regular action of the mind; that, moreover, certain kindred notions enter into the daily cult of them all; in short, that, between the Saktist and the ordinary Hindu, the difference is one of degree and not of kind, and that in all the race there exist those germs of mental and moral maladies which, in certain sects, are seen in chronic form and of intentional development.

Now these are souls strangely constituted, disturbed, perverted, vitiated from their birth. Into these souls, moreover, there now fall, by chance and in abundance, general ideas from all quarters, like seeds of disease falling into an organism already unsound. Thousands of young Hindus prepare for the examinations which admit to a public career; and they fill the numerous universities of India. They study Sanskrit, Persian, Arabic, the old Asiatic philosophies, two or three literatures. They are penetrated with the English ideas which are in the air, everywhere about them. In the higher classes, their professors are Englishmen. From their earliest school days, Addison and Macaulay have been their classics. Later, they attack the philosophers, Hamilton or Spencer. They read English reviews and journals; here they find literary and political essays, miscellaneous news, statistics, reports of every kind, which describe in detail, dissect, classify, catalogue all the countless forms of English life — intellectual or moral, artistic or religious, commercial or social. The novel gives them English types of character — labourers, clergymen, sailors, young girls, squires, business men; and under all these forms lies a conception of life, religion, duty, love, death — not merely that of another race, but of another human nature. Not only are these young Hindus nourished upon foreign ideas, but they live the life of a foreign soul, which thinks, feels, desires, in a manner contrary to their own. It is an operation which must cause anxiety, this infusion of another blood; and it may result, like the crossing of very distinct animal species, in the production of monstrosities which cannot live.

This morning, on the river bank, these thoughts occurred to me while I was exchanging a few words with a young Brahman whose intelligent and amiable face had much impressed me. This youth is a pupil in an English school in Benares, and expects to enter the university at Allahabad, in preparation for the Civil Service. He has read Addison; he is to study the Upanishads. Meantime he is preparing for the mathematical examinations. The question of India for India came up; he is interested in the congress of Allahabad, which asks for an autonomous parliament. At the same time, he belongs to a caste which he must not quit; he worships the Hindu gods, pronounces the syllable OM in their honour; he holds his breath; he offers flowers to the sacred cows as part of his customary devotions. It must be, of course, that European culture tends to destroy his hereditary faith in all these rites; but let us not forget that he lives among Hindu cults, that every morning he sees the multitude devoutly splashing in the river, and the Brahmans figuring with their fingers the hundred and eight incarnations of Vishnu; that the first words he ever heard, those which he still hears most frequently, are religious formulas, sacred syllables, Vedic texts, and extracts from the Puranas; that, in his presence, his father worships the five black stones, a bell, a vase; and that this spectacle, incessantly repeated, imprints on the very depths of his being a stamp, upon which neither reading nor reasoning can have the slightest effect; and that, hence, all which seems to us so extraordinary appears to him natural, and those ideas which to us are contradictory of each other in his mind belong together. It is an astonishing intellectual and moral structure, too different from our own to be to us sympathetically conceivable. With much erudition, a European mind may be flexible enough to reproduce for itself the ideas and sentiments, the sequences of images and emotions, which formed the soul of a mediæval monk or of an Athenian architect. This is because, in spite of the passage of centuries, they are not altogether strangers to us; it is because they make part of the same human group with ourselves; it is because they were on the path of that slow evolution which has now reached us—the historic wave which at this moment lifts us into the light; they had their share in giving it its direction and its form. The vital sap which circulates in the European of to-day passed through them, as that which nourishes a topmost leaf was elaborated in the dark roots. Something of them survives, and makes part of the accumulated inheritance which the European generations hand down; for the present contains all the past. Some few men can understand a Greek temple or a prayer of the ninth century. Who of us can really feel a Purana, or a Hindu edifice? Granted that there was once a certain tie of blood between us and these Indian peoples, the crossing with black races, the secular action of a different climate and different natural phenomena, have destroyed it. Their soul is a composite of a mysterious kind, not only beyond our experience, but outside of what is possible for us to comprehend. We note its manifestations, we perceive the externals—physiognomies, gestures, rites, prayers, style, art, customs. The substance of the soul is impenetrable.

This afternoon, some expeditions hither and yon in Benares. For a very few rupees, I have a barouche with two horses, a coachman, groom, and a *peon* who accompanies the carriage, running with admirable gravity. These people are naturally silent, serious, with unchanging faces. The trotting peon, in his tight red tunic, who clears the crowd before us, is absorbed in the gravity of his function. His elbows held close in, his chest dilated, his head high, he runs—now and then ejaculating a sharp, short cry.

The division of labour is carried to a great extreme here; there must be the coachman to drive, the groom to open the carriage door, the peon to clear the road. A European in India must submit to all this display. It would be monstrous for him to go on foot, or to carry a package! An English officer must not go from one place to another without a whole caravan of men and luggage in his train. Last year in London, I heard a corporal relating that in India he would ring for his servant to pick up a handkerchief. Many gentlemen keep a man specially to take care of their pipes. The house of a civilian requires fifty servants; there are tailors, bakers, washermen, not to mention a crowd of people who come every morning for the day's work. Thus at Rome, the patrician had his army of servitors, clients, and freedmen. The white man is here the master, the noble, and many believe him a sorcerer. Secretly, however, he is despised, as ceremonially impure, polluted by the daily use of liquors and meats. In contrast to this serious, quiet, and wily race, he appears coarse, with his noisy laughter, his athletic sports, his many requirements, his vigorous movements, his activity always conspicuous. His wife, seen in the streets unveiled, outrages all decency. In the scale of being, he ranks far below the Sudra; a Hindu must have committed many and odious sins to return to earth as a European. At the same time, terror and respect prostrate the Indian before his white master, who seems omnipotent with his strength of muscle, with his wealth, his weapons, and his mysterious inventions. What does the Hindu think of these iron threads stretched across the country, or of this black veil under which we put our heads, taking aim with a mysterious box at some edifice? This morning, for nothing in the world would my boatmen touch a piece of my photographic apparatus. My "boy" awaits my orders, bent nearly double, his arms crossed on his breast, as if he were a slave. All Sepoys present arms to the European traveller. You respond with condescension, half scornful, just moving the head, and fall back in your barouche, which, for thirty cents the first hour, and twelve for the subsequent hours, carries you at a gallop from palace to palace, from marvel to marvel.

It is well to accept one's vocation of tourist, and follow your guide with docility. Mine, who has traditions, takes me to the bank of the Ganges, and we cross the river on a barge. This brings us to the palace of the Maharajah. Three broad marble courts give access to the grand hall, furnished with a luxury too conspicuous, half Hindu, half European.

There is nothing to see here except the gallery of portraits, the ancestors of His Highness, all Kshatriyas, of the warrior race, the true Aryan conquerors of India, very stiff, very pompous, in their full white robes, one hand on the heart, holding flowers; or else armed with the strange weapon used in the tiger-hunt. One ancestor standing, his chest well thrown out, like the king in a comic opera, his arm extended and one finger on the head of a large cane —recalling the attitude of Rigaud's Louis XIV.—his beard spread wide on both sides of the face, poses, with a braggart lordliness and an air of consummate coxcombry. At his side, upon the same wall, the Prince of Wales, very swell and very insipid; and a portrait of the winner of the Derby in 1865, the great, meagre, classic horse, with his minute jockey in the yellow silk cap; old chromolithographs that you will see in any English inn, but precious *bibelots* here in India, and framed accordingly.

This rajah, who gives a hundred rupees daily to support the sacred cows and to keep up the temple of Siva, was present in 1887 at the Queen's Jubilee in England. It is said he was much impressed by what he saw at that time, but chiefly by the great height of the English horses.

Opposite, on the other side of the Ganges, in the vast crowd of edifices that border the river, is the temple of the monkeys. There they are, the tawny gods, frisking over the porticos, or hanging by the tail from the notches in the stonework. At sight of us, a great tumult, a great tremor of curiosity; with supple leaps they gather, chattering, winking, scanning our faces with their anxious, piercing eyes. Piously I make my offering, some grain bought of the Brahman who guards the entrance to the temple; at once an angry whining, sharp outcries, a scramble of hairy bodies, a confusion of sinuous backs.

As may be supposed, these divinities are not in confinement, like the monkeys of the Jardin des Plantes. The temple is merely their headquarters, whence they sally out every morning to infest the city, pillaging the houses and gardens. An Englishman killed some of them who were stealing his fruit; thereupon there was great uproar in Benares; he was besieged in his own house, and it was necessary to call out the Sepoys to protect him.

On Wednesday is the great monkey feast; almost all of the sacred band remain in their temple. Devotees come in crowds and bring offerings—grain, cocoanuts, and fruits. A goat is solemnly sacrificed; an exciting spectacle, which makes the hairy crests stand on end, the teeth chatter, and the eyebrows draw together in a frown above the sharp little eyes.

It is proper to visit the Hindu University; for

this Benares is a very ancient centre of Indian culture. Of old its teachers philosophised, and students came from afar to receive instruction in their doctrines. Astronomy, which contemplates the eternal skies, was also much in honour here. This morning I visited an ancient observatory, full of mysterious instruments of stone, covered with strange writings; and my mind reverted to those obscure ages when this city, unknown to our Europe, elaborated that old Oriental science whereby the inquisitive Brahmans were able to calculate the sun's declination, and the revolution of the stars around the pole.

Sanskrit has continued to be the language of the pandits here. They use it as the professors of certain Swedish universities to this day write in Latin. At Benares, the old sacred texts are constantly explained and commented upon: the Vedas, the great epics, the Upanishads, the Puranas; some of these Brahmans are known to our European Orientalists.

The English call Benares the Oxford of India, and the university building which they have erected seems brought from Oxford. To see these arches, these square, crenellated towers, these portals, these niches, these clusters of slender colonnettes, you would think yourself at the doors of Oriel or Magdalen. Only instead of the old granite, all exfoliated by time and weather, all stamped with the sadness of the wan sky, this is a stone glittering with light, impenetrated with the felicity and mildness of the blue ether. For surroundings, instead of monotonous lawns and the fine, tremulous foliage of the English trees, there are tall, stiff, lustrous palms. Within, under the pointed arcades, there are groups of students gathered around their professors. But these are not the blond, bold heads that you have seen at Oxford in a hall so similar to this; fat, gentle, effeminate, Oriental faces, and slender figures draped in soft garments. The pandit Bapu-Deva-Sastri, professor of mathematics, is my guide, and the young men salute us as we enter, with a graceful inclination of the body, the eyes downcast, lifting their clasped hands to their lips, with a repeated gesture. Before a blackboard covered with algebraic symbols, boys are seated cross-legged; on their heads are velvet caps wrought with gold; the oval faces, the long eyelashes, the colourless complexions, the beautiful curve of the lips, have an enchanting gentleness and seriousness.

Further on, older students are occupied with a lesson in philosophy; two books lie on the pandit's table; they are Mansel's "Philosophy," and Herbert Spencer's "Social Statics."

It is difficult to see anything in Benares beyond the streets and the public buildings. Letters of introduction give you access only to European homes; and of the Hindu world you can see scarcely beyond its exterior. However, leaving at this point my guide and his catalogued lists of "sights," I was able to visit two Indian houses. The first is that of the babu Devi-Parshad, dealer in cloth of gold and silver; little, white, cool rooms, with very low ceilings, and entirely without furniture. The stone walls, adorned with carvings and painted flowers, are recessed in square niches where abide red gods —quadrupeds with human faces, the monstrous Ganesa, patron of commerce as well as of literature. Above the gods, English diplomas, awards of expositions, as you would see them in a Parisian office.

At the end of the last room, padlocked doors, which a lad opens for our gratification, keep secure the riches of the house—fantastic stuffs woven of precious metal, laces like cobwebs, marvellous silks of the "Thousand and One Nights," sun-colour, moon-colour, which are cautiously displayed before us. In the centre of the room, on a pile of cushions, is enthroned the master of the house, effeminate and nonchalant of face. Seated amid the silks which cover him, he is taking his music lesson, and from his long guitar rise the Oriental ritornelles, complicated, dissonant, sad, and eternally the same.

On the ground, in a corner, a scribe, in a great green robe, is bent over books filled with cabalistic writings. An old, shaven face, thin, compressed lips, an aquiline nose supporting spectacles, the intelligent and austere countenance of an Alsatian schoolmaster. He shows me his sacred cord, which proves him to be a Brahman; I have already seen among men of his caste faces singularly European. Just now, on the shore of the Ganges, a young man had the prematurely old, thin, fatigued features of a Parisian student. Strange power of type, that thousands of years are powerless to destroy — the same in a Roman bust, in the *flâneur* of a Parisian boulevard, in a Brahman of Benares.

While the babu winds his eternal, plaintive scale, this old scribe, who seems very learned, demonstrates to me the relationship between English and Sanskrit. He brings together the words *pitar* and father, *bhratar* and brother, *duhitar* and daughter— well-known parallels which are to-day in all our grammars, but very impressive here, in the mouth of a worshipper of Siva, who looks like one of our own people.

Then, we go to see the dancing-girls. Their dwelling is in the heart of the city, in the most populous street, in the midst of the bazaar. This endless streaming of the motley crowd, these figures of all colours, this confusion of nudities and floating garments, is always surprising. In the middle of the street the human current flows more freely; on the side-walks, rows of men are seated, carving in copper, stamping bronze; merchants are busy with their account-books; others, sitting on the ground negligently abandon their black heads to the barber.

The street is tortuous, very narrow between the projecting booths, which extend out from the houses, crowded with fruit, with copper ware, with jewelry of coloured glass, and embroidered slippers; and it is still further narrowed above one's head by a confusion of terraces, balconies, statuettes, verandas, and wooden galleries, which notch the irregular strip of sky. It is an interior of the Oriental ant-hill, unchanged in centuries. Such must be "the quarter of the shops" in Bagdad of familiar tales!

My "boy" opens a little door which he knows well, and we step into the half-light of a low hall, surrounded by a quadrilateral of slender colonnettes. There is no one here: only three stout little gods sit, half visible, in their niches. At the end of the hall a dark staircase, up which we grope our way. On the floor above, we are in the abode of the dancing-girls. It is dark, and the air is close, in this great room, with its thick carpet and walls hung with embroidered silk. For furniture, there are cushions; and from the ceiling hangs a very rich chandelier, extending in innumerable branches, tufty, as all Hindu things are. The atmosphere is perfumed and makes one giddy. On the floor are vases loaded with the inevitable yellow flowers, and there are perfume boxes, whence rise, in spirals, the blue vapours of incense.

Now we see that it is inhabited, this silent chamber we had thought empty. Seated on the carpets, resting their elbows upon a balustrade, three women are looking idly down into the street. Our entrance has not aroused them from their torpor; scarcely have they so much as turned their heads. Bronzed faces, very pure outlines, the eyelids and eyelashes singularly long, great black eyes surcharged with languor and voluptuousness; yet serious, and with a certain dignity which is not at all impaired by the nose jewel.

This immobility, this seriousness, this Oriental silence, are always disconcerting. Thus they pass their days, idly reclining, wrapped in their draperies, half asleep in the darkness of this hall, where the perfumed vapours rise and are diffused, watching through the fretwork of the carved wooden balcony the crowds that are streaming past in the narrow street below; but themselves always hidden, invisible from without. Sometimes they make bouquets, they amuse themselves with their flowers, or one of them takes her guitar, and the dark room is filled with the rapid scratching of the strings—minor scales of a strange rhythm, indefinitely repeated, curiously involved, ceasing on notes which are not final, which make you expect something further, a music strange and monotonous as their life. This is the existence of all Hindu women cloistered in the zenanas. A life like this should produce souls of an extreme simplicity; but why are these faces so wonderfully serious, and the great dark eyes full of a passion so concentrated?

Enters silently a tall, sly Hindu, who talks long and low with my guide. It appears that it is very expensive—a nautch—one must pay a hundred rupees for it. As I hesitate upon this, it is explained to me that the dancing-girls will be attired in precious stuffs, costumes which have cost thousands of rupees : the coffers containing these festal garments are brought for me to see. Indeed the boxes are full of most beautiful things : Benares silks, all stiff with silver stars, delicate gauzes on which quiver specks of gold laces embroidered with jewels and with the burnished wings of scarabs. The thousand lamps of the great chandelier will be lighted, and the dance lasts the whole night through.

It is a strange pleasure—the greatest possible, according to the Hindus. There is no festival, no solemnity, without its nautch. When a European of importance arrives at Calcutta or Bombay, the great native functionaries invite him to witness this, and expend vast sums to show him four dancing-girls. The European invariably tires; to all Englishmen who have seen it, this spectacle is an incomprehensible amusement. The foreigner accepts from courtesy, and goes away after an hour, sprinkled with the perfumes, wreathed with the flowers that every host owes to his guest. The Hindu men remain, seated like so many Buddhas, cross-legged, their hands clasped, mute and motionless; and so the entire night passes. Observe that there is nothing sensual in the classic nautch; and, compared with this dance, the most innocent of our ballets would seem free. The women are loaded with draperies; the more beautiful the stuffs, the more expensive the nautch. Who shall explain the slow intoxication, the beatified drowsiness, the vague torpor, the somnolent, subtle charm which seizes upon these Hindu men, sitting in a row upon their heels? The tinkling guitar goes on repeating the same sad and confused phrase; the garments of the dancing-girls flash iridescent hues; the draperies whirl together, then separate; the gems scintillate;

the arms are slowly extended; the body swings to and fro, or stops suddenly, motionless, in a prolonged shiver, of a vibration almost imperceptible; heads are thrown back as if swooning, wrists writhe, fingers stiffen and quiver; the cithern goes on repeating its slender, melancholy phrase; and the hours fly. It is a pleasure analogous to our own in following the slow, graceful curling of a puff of cigar smoke, or the gentle motion of a procession of white clouds against the blue of a summer's sky. The *Me* is lost for the moment, scattered into space; there is nothing left but the rhythmic scintillation of those precious stones, the soft undulation of that smoke, the gentle and splendid movement of those clouds.

Such is my poor attempt at explanation. Exterior resemblances to our modes of being do not reveal to us what passes in the interior of these souls. What effort of intelligence or of sympathy, for instance, could make us understand the fact I am about to mention? On the 15th of July 1857, Nana Sahib gave orders to massacre the English prisoners. The men having been shot in the open air, the women and children, crowded in a bungalow, were destroyed by repeated firing through the windows. At the end of an hour, the cries within having ceased, Nana caused the dead and the dying to be brought out, and to be thrown into a deep well. That evening the sahib ordered a nautch, and reposing upon a sofa, he passed the night satiating his eyes with the sinuous and serpentine movements of four dancing-girls.

I did not go to see the nautch, finding it decidedly too expensive. Besides, my curiosity was somewhat blunted. Instead, I passed the evening at the hotel, upon the verandah, lying in a *chaise longue*, my "boy" at my side, on the ground, wrapped in his rug. How calm and splendid is the night, broadened by the moonlight which filters through the green masses of the palms, and projects short and well-defined shadows of all the plants! Overhead, two little silvery clouds repose alone; and at times the thin, far-off cry of an insect renders the silence more profound.

In the slow smoke of the Egyptian tobacco float to and fro many things which I have seen to-day; many images, as yet well defined, but destined to lose their colour, to disappear gradually, to fall into the *no more*. In the nocturnal peace of this solitary garden, after all the fatiguing daylight, after all the tumult of the Asiatic multitude, how easy to sink into the reverie of the ancient Brahmans! This noisy world, these luminous visions which have followed one another through the last eighteen hours, how it all appears a dream, an exciting dream, from which one awakens to find one's self tranquil, and so alone in the silence of this broad night! A dream, the vast river which flowed this morning, shining and muddy, past the rose-coloured temples; a dream, the black and white multitude swarming on the bank, the wilderness of temples and chapels, the narrow streets beaten hard by the naked feet of the Asiatic crowd. It is difficult to conceive that, at this moment, in this resonant air of night, the solitary river is whispering and rustling obscurely on the marble stairs from which the crowd has gone away. There is no longer a person there in the presence of the great river. The two hundred and fifty thousand inhabitants of Benares, having quitted the streets, are stretched out upon their braided mats. The Brahmans are at rest from their ceremonial observances. The two thousand and fifty-four temples are empty, and the rays of the moon light up the innumerable chapels now deserted, in which the bronze bulls and all the ancient idols are now left alone. Yes, it is difficult to believe that all this is real,—river, palace, people, idols,—occupying its point of space on a vast globe, eighteen hundred leagues in radius, covered in many other places with other human mildew; and that this globe—bathed on its other side in sunshine, here, in the paler light of this gentle planet—is revolving very rapidly and noiselessly in space!

I have before me two sacred pictures which I bought this morning in a booth. They are very childish; they are rude, and yet carefully finished. The paint, which is used very thick, is applied upon a layer of plaster with which the paper is covered. The personages are represented in profile, but the eyes are as if in a front view, like the ancient mural paintings of Egypt.

The first represents a beatified Brahman seated on the ground; his plump body half naked, his hands clasped upon his crossed legs, his rosary around his neck, girt with the thread of the twice-born; he is looking upon the ground. The head is shaven, the brow bent forward, marked with three horizontal lines; the moustache white and heavy; the eyes half closed. There is nothing Oriental in the face, which might be that of a German professor. Only the development of the cranium is enormous, and the expression of immobility is striking. It appears that this man has been dreaming thus for a very long time, and that he will never arouse himself. All around is a vague green expanse, ending far off in the red of the sky. The man is alone in the immensity of the country.

The second picture is finer, illuminated in crimson and gold. A Brahman reposes beneath the palms of a forest, his legs folded under him upon a rug and draped in yellow drawers; he is still more plump than the other, with the same soft, inert flesh, which lies in folds and fat ridges. The face, less dull, is not weighed down by meditation, but lighted with serene beatitude. One of his bare arms disappears within the red bag, where his fingers make the sacred figures; the other holds daintily, between the thumb and fore-finger, a white lotus flower. A golden halo proclaims him freed from future migrations, for ever absorbed in Brahma; at his feet his disciple, in the white robe of a neophyte, with hands respectfully clasped together, listens, kneeling.

What are they, the solemn words that the blessed one is speaking under the green roof of the palms? The Upanishads tell us what they are; and this evening, as I turn over the leaves of the sacred books, I seem to understand my two pictures: I can follow the meditation of my first Brahman; I can hear the religious discourse of the master to his pupil.

The recluse meditates, his eyes half closed, his massive head inclined toward the ground :—

"Hari! Om! This light shining above the sky, higher than all else, in the highest world, beyond which there is no other :

"This light is also the light which is in man.

"All things are Brahma. I meditate upon this visible world as beginning, as ending, as breathing in Brahma.

"This Intelligence whose body is spirit, whose form is light, whose thoughts are true, whose nature is like the ether, omnipresent and invisible, from whom proceed all works, all desires, all sweet perfumes; he who envelops all things, who never speaks, who is never understood :

"He is also the Me within my heart, smaller than a grain of rice, smaller than a mustard seed, smaller than the kernel of a mustard seed;

"He is also the Me within my heart, greater than the earth, greater than the sky, greater than all worlds.

"As fire, the element, after it has entered the world, while remaining one, becomes many, according to what it burns; so the one Existence at the bottom of all things becomes diverse, according to that which he penetrates, and he also exists without, in appearances of things.

"He is the eternal thinker, whose thoughts are

not eternal ; who, although himself but one, satisfies the desires of all. The wise, who recognise him in the depth of their own Me, eternal peace is with them, but not with others.

"In him does not shine the sun, nor the moon, nor the stars, nor the lightning, still less this fire. When he shines, all shines after him ; by his light all things are enlightened. . . .

"Beyond the world is the Undeveloped ; beyond the Undeveloped, there is nothing ; this is the end, the limit.

"This Being is concealed in all things, and is not visible on the outside, but the subtle seers perceive him by their acute and subtle intelligence.

"He who has known That which no man can hear, or touch, or taste, or feel; which has no form, which does not pass away, eternal, without beginning, without end, unalterable ; that man is saved from the jaws of death.

"The wise man who knows this Being, as bodiless among bodies, as immutable among things that change, as omnipresent, this wise man is freed from grief.

"But he who is not calm and subdued, whose spirit is not in tranquillity, he will never know this Being.

"Who knows where he dwells, He to whom Brahmans and Kshatriyas are only food,[*] to whom death itself is but an aliment ?"

Thus goes on the reverie of the recluse, on his way toward the perfect condition. He has not yet

[*] In whom are absorbed the races and generations.

attained it, for he thinks; and immobility is not yet established in his brain. When the five "instruments of knowledge" (the five senses) are inert, when the mind acts no longer, then the man is delivered. Then the qualified Brahmá which is himself, enfranchised from mode, change, and illusion, again becomes the neuter Bráhmă, the absolute, "which is neither cause nor effect, nor this nor that, nor past nor future." Formerly, polluted by ignorance, the man manifested himself in appearances. Now "he is as pure water poured into pure water, remaining the same." As a wave of the sea, losing its form and its impulse, sinks into the sombre depths of the motionless waters; so the man, emptied of the desires and emotions and thoughts which made up his personality, sinks, disappears, in the calm, black depths of being.

This is the same doctrine which the Brahman with the golden halo, seated under the palm-trees, unveils to his kneeling disciple, and the following story,* also from the old Upanishads, may serve as a commentary upon my second picture :—

"Hari! Om! In those days lived Svetaketu Aruneya. His father Uddalaka said to him: 'Svetaketu, go now to school, for there is no one of our race, my beloved, who, not having studied the Vedas, is Brahman by race only.'

"Having begun his training at the age of twelve, Svetaketu returned to his father when he was

---

* The word Upanishad indicates, according to Max Müller, the attitude of the disciple, with hands clasped, and eyes fixed upon his master.

twenty-four, having studied the Vedas, vain, believing himself very learned, and proud.

"His father said to him : 'Svetaketu, since thou art so vain, hast thou ever sought that instruction whereby we learn to hear what is not audible, to see what is invisible, to understand that which is incomprehensible?'

"'What is this instruction, my lord?' the young man asked.

"The father replied : 'My dear son, as, from a piece of earth, we know all earth—diversities being but names and arising from language, the truth being that all these things are earth—likewise, my dear son, is that which we learn by this instruction.'

"The son said : 'Surely these venerable men know it not. For if they had known, why should they not have taught it to me? Instruct me then, my lord !'

"'So be it,' said the father.

"Then, in the forest, the disciple kneels, clasps his hands, and remains motionless. The father, seated on the ground, holding in his left hand the slender stem of the lotus, speaks as follows :—

"'In the beginning, my dear son, there was only that which is, that alone and nothing second.

"'Others say that in the beginning there was only that which is not, alone ; and that from that which is not came forth that which is.

"'But how could this be so, my dear son ? How could that which is come forth from that which is not ? No ; only that which existed in the beginning; that only, and nothing second (that is to say, since there is something rather than nothing, being exists from all eternity).

"'And That thought: "May I be many! May I extend myself!" And from him came forth fire.

"'And the fire thought: "May I become many! May I spread!" And from it came forth water.

"'This is why we see that when a man is warm, he perspires. For water appears upon his body and it comes from fire.

"'And the water thought: "May I become many! May I spread!" And from the water came forth earth, all solid things, and food.'"

In the five subsequent Khandas, the disciple learns that all things are made from the union of fire, water, and earth. "In these things also man has his root. 'By means of digested food, this scion, the body, is formed and grows. And what could be its root except the earth and food? And since earth and food are scions, seek their root. It is water. And the root of water is fire. And the fire is also a scion. And its root is the True One.

"'Yes, all things have their root and dwelling-place, and place of rest in the True One.

"'When a man leaves this world, his speech is absorbed into his mind, his mind into his breath, his breath into heat, heat into the most elevated of beings.

"'And this thing, this subtle essence, the root of all—in this, all that exists has its being. It is the True. It is the Being; and thou thyself, O Svetaketu! art this Being.'

"'My lord, deign to instruct me further,' said the son.

"'So be it,' the father answered.

"'The rivers, my son, flow, some to the east, as the Ganges, others to the west, as the Sindhu.

"'They go from the sea to the sea (that is, they rise from it as clouds, and return to it as rivers). They again become truly the sea. And as these rivers, when they are in the sea, no longer say: "I am this river, or I am that river"; so, my son, all creatures, when they go forth out of the True, know not that they go forth out of the True.

"'In this thing, this subtle essence, all that exists has its being. It is the True, it is Being, and thou thyself, O Svetaketu, art this Being.'

"'My lord, deign to instruct me further,' says the son.

"'So be it,' replies the father.*

"'A man was carried away from his own country by robbers. His eyes being bandaged, he was led into a forest, full of terrors and dangers. And not knowing where he was, he began to weep, hoping to be delivered from his bonds. Then a passer-by had pity upon him, cut his bonds, and sent him back, rejoicing, to his own country.

"'Our country is Being, the king of the world. This body, made of three elements, fire, water, and earth, subject to cold and heat, is a forest in which we wander. And the bandages upon our eyes are our desires for many things, real and unreal, our wives, our children, our cattle; and the robbers

* Here the text has been expanded by a commentator.

who have brought us into this forest are our actions. (The actions of preceding life which have caused us transmigration, instead of the absorption into Brahma.)

" 'Then we weep, and we say : " I am the son of such a one, I am happy, I am sad, I am foolish, I am wise, I am righteous, I have been born, I die." These are the bonds which fetter us (individuality). Sometimes we meet a man who knows the Me of Brahma, and whose bonds have been broken. He has pity on us, and instructs us that we are not the son of such a one, that we are not happy or sad, wise or foolish, that we have not been born and do not die, but are only That which Is.

" ' In this thing, this subtle essence, all that exists has its being. It is the Being, the True, and thou thyself, O Svetaketu ! art this Being.'

" And Svetaketu understood what his father said ; yes, he understood it.

" And knowing him who is one, who animates all germs, in whom all unites and all separates, the adorable lord, the dispenser of benefits, Svetaketu *entered for ever into peace.*"

This pantheism, which was taught for two thousand years, is not the doctrine of an isolated thinker or of a school. It describes in philosophic language the special *vision* of the world which, more or less clear, has been that of all this race. To understand it, observe the spirit of another human variety, and, together with these old philosophic poems of the Brahmans, read the Bible. What do you find there ? It is lyric poetry : angers, despairs, enthusiasms, hatreds, violent emotions, shocks of all kinds ; all possible feelings of the soul, expressed in brusque metaphors and brilliant imagery, in an abrupt style, in a simple language, incapable of following the undulations of speculative thought, but exactly made to render an emotion by a cry. Now, what is the effect upon man of lasting and vehement emotion, but to cause him to fall back upon his own thoughts ? When he suffers, when he hates, he is occupied altogether with himself ; he perceives himself as distinct from the exterior world which causes him suffering. In an emotional soul, the coherent Me declares itself, stands alone ; and when the man essays to conceive of that which stands behind all things, he conceives of it also as a *Me*, distinct and omnipotent.

With these Brahmans the opposite faculties have arrived at opposite results. What do we find in the Vedas ? Poems upon Nature, hymns to the Sun, the Rain, the Clouds, Fire, the Sky, the Earth, the Wind, the Storm, the Dawn of Day. No subjective personal poetry. Instead of permanent emotions, there is a changeful play of images. The soul is no longer a distinct being, but a reflection of nature, a changeful reflection of its events which change. It becomes the cloud floating in the blue ; it becomes the sun which rises in the East. When an emotion penetrates the soul, it does but pass through it. It does not remain ; it does not develop slowly into interior, concentrated passion. It is at once projected beyond the man himself, who thus lends to the external world his ever-changing and fleeting emotions. If he is joyous, it is the gaiety of Agni, sparkling amid the vine branches; if he is timorous, it is the timidity of the Auroras veiling themselves in cloud, like blushing girls. In short, instead of concentrating himself in one substance—a Me, who wills, acts, bleeds, cries out—the Vedic poet is scattered abroad through the world; he diffuses himself in *things*, his soul is filled with the forms, sounds, colours of nature, and nature is animated with his thoughts and desires.

These living and divine forces of nature he adores; but there is something peculiar in his polytheism. Indra, Varuna, Agni, Surya are souls, elemental souls—not rigidly shut into a few fixed attributes, not conceived of as distinct, unchanging personalities, but varying, floating, capable of reciprocal transformations. This Aurora is also the Sun, the Sun is also Fire, Fire is also Lightning, Lightning is Tempest, Tempest is Rain. Varuna becomes Agni, Agni becomes Surya. They all unite, blend, mutually interpenetrate. There is no permanence, either in the human person, who does not conceive of himself as a person, or in the external world, which is all change. Nothing remains in the whole universe but a whirl of ephemeral thoughts and forms, an ever-flowing stream. The germ of this conception is in the Vedas, but it is in the old philosophic poems of the Brahmans that it grows, matures, and attains its full development. In reading these poems, we are stupefied at the discovery that the most rooted of our European notions, the idea of the *me-substance*, does not exist for them. To understand such a mental condition as this we need to recall certain rare and very fugitive moments of our own lives. Every man knows those moments of morbid dream in which the *me* seems to melt away. One speaks his own name aloud, and it seems to be a meaningless sound, designating no one; one questions anxiously, "Is there any *myself?*" "What does it mean, *myself?*"

This strange sensation, with us so transient, is permanent with them. Their personality appears to them only as a point where visions cross each other; they feel nothing permanent within themselves. Everything about them is transient, and the doctrine of the universal flow becomes systematic: "The body comes from food, that is to say, from the earth; it attracts to itself external elements," rejects them and attracts others; thus it grows, and subsists, in a life made up of changes. That their enumerations heap together "water, sky, earth, ether, fire, birds, grass, trees, worms, moths, ants, thoughts, abstractions, the Vedas," is due to the consideration that all these things blend in the universal whirl. As these vapours exhaled from the soil, the sea, animals, plants—which, just now, were a part of the soil, the sea, the animal, the plant—are mingled, rise, are lighted up in the sky, float, traverse space at random, grow cool, fall, and, as chance wills, become once more soil, sea, plant, animal, things thus unite and separate which we believe to be distinct. "The priest, having become air, becomes smoke; having become smoke, he becomes fog; having become fog, he becomes cloud, and falls in rain. Then he returns into life as corn, rice, grass, tree, millet."

Between this view and pantheism there is but a step; and this step they take in two ways. Since all forms pass, and do but *appear*, they are illusory. If we take away qualities and modes of being, what remains? "Nothing," say the Buddhists, "*Nada;* the world is not; nothingness is the only reality." "*That which is*," says the orthodox Brahmans; that which is, and of which nothing more can be said than *it is;* the *that*, void of all quality; which is neither this nor that, neither cause nor effect; in short, the neuter Bráhmă, indeterminate, undeveloped, "which thinks not, wills not, sees not, knows not,"—Being, pure and abstract. On the surface of this neuter Bráhmă, which is attained by pure thought, is the masculine Brahmá, living, tangible, having colour. For, after considering the one substance which is hidden under the whirl of forms, one may consider the power which organises and keeps up this whirl. Since all is motion in the world, there is a power which guides this motion. Since the world is not inert like a stone, but living, like a tree,* there is a soul which sustains and develops it. This soul is Brahmá, the universal germ, "the living and incarnate Me." Since he is living, he has qualities, and is not the same with the neuter Bráhmă, of which he is only the first manifestation. He is Brahma, but Brahma now veiled

* A favourite metaphor with the Brahmans. Often the world is designated by the single word, "the tree."

by the illusory Maya, Brahma subjected to time. "There are two forms of Brahma : *he who knows time, and he who knows not time:* he who knows time has parts. Time matures and dissolves all beings in the great Me, the living soul; but he who knows in what time itself is absorbed, he comprehends the Vedas."

We must conceive, then, in the beginning and at the root of all things, the absolute Being, pure and void, which is at the bottom of all forms and all germs. Developing itself outward, it is subjected to Maya, *illusion.* "Like a spider wrapped in threads drawn from her own substance, it assumes qualities coming from itself," and its first projection is the living Brahmá, the soul, or subtle and universal idea, "which acts within the world and diversifies it. This soul is neither male nor female, yet neither is it neuter." This it is, which, "becoming this and that," takes millions of ephemeral forms, all emerging from itself, all falling back into it; itself fugitive, like all this visible universe, and condemned, after these myriads of millions of centuries which to Brahma are as a day, to be absorbed in the neuter Being "which has neither shadows, nor body, nor colour."

Let it be conceived that the world is an immense tree, solidly rooted in the ground. Whence do they come, these innumerable leaves that rustle in the wind, that glisten in the light, these widespread branches, this delicious fruit, this solid column of a trunk, ever growing stronger, all this lustrous and perfumed vegetation ? They come from a primitive germ, now diffused, but still vital and active, alike in the deep, dark roots and in the impalpable dust which gives the petal of the flower its colour and smoothness. Bark, leaves, flowers, cells, all change —they die and are renewed, like everything in the world. But the primitive force which reared the tree subsists through all these deaths and births; gives their form and their order to the ever new and fleeting elements. Whence, then, does it come, this active force which is like the living Brahmá that animates the universe? From the soil, the inert ground, of which one day a portion became organic. This soil is the image of the primitive Bráhmă; from it all proceeds; to it all returns; and when, after centuries, the force which sustains the tree shall be exhausted, changes ceasing, development being arrested, the tree will return to the earth, and again all will be motionless.

"At this moment, thou art a woman, a man, a child, a young girl, an old man leaning upon a staff; thou art born with thy face turned on all sides. Thou art the blue honey-bee, the red-eyed green parrot; thou art the thunder-cloud, the seasons; thou art the seas. Thou art without beginning, being infinite, thou of whom all worlds are born. But as the flowing rivers which go toward the ocean are absorbed and swallowed up in it, losing their names and their forms, so the sun and moon, the Kshatriyas and Brahmans, mosquitos, bees, flamingos, the devas, Vishnu, Siva, and time itself in which lives the second Brahmá, will be absorbed in the inconceivable existence, and their names and their forms will be no more." And in reality, at this moment they are not, these forms; they are only appearances. Brahma, regarding himself in the mirror of time and of illusion, perceives himself as multiple and mutable, but in reality there is only *that which is*.

This is no mere theory, no scholastic thesis, no philosophy framed by idle speculation, but an active, practical, deeply-rooted belief, elaborated by solitary and concentrated meditation. Thrown back upon himself, absorbed in reflection, the Brahman no longer distinguishes the real world from that of his dreams, and sees it floating to and fro like a vapour. Hence the tie which attaches him to this world has no strength. How can a man love that which is known to be unreal? Why seek to grasp what must inevitably slip from the hand?

"O holy one! what profits it to be happy in this vile and fragile body, an accumulation of bones and blood and skin, of nerves, marrow, flesh, tears? What profits it to be happy in this body, which is assailed by hatred, covetousness, envy, deception, fear, anguish, jealousy, the separation from friends, hunger, thirst, old age, death, disease, suffering? And we see that all is perishable, flies and moths and other insects, grass and trees, which grow up and decay. Look back toward those who are no more; look forward to those who as yet are not. Men ripen like grain, they perish; and, like grain, they spring up anew. There have been powerful men, strong to draw the bow, chiefs of the people, Sudyama, Asvapati, Sasabindu, and kings, who, with their families about them, have abandoned their great felicity, and gone forth out of this life; and what has become of them? The great oceans dry up, the mountains fall, *the polar star changes its place*, the earth will be submerged, the gods also will pass away. In a world like this, why desire to be happy? Oh, bend toward me! In this world I languish, as a frog in a dry well!"

Thus the King Krihadhrata bewailed himself, who, cutting off the root of desire in his heart, had taken refuge in the forest. For a thousand years he remained there, with lifted arms, looking at the sun, motionless like his brethren, the gymnosophists, who sit solitary in the Indian jungles. For to immobility all Hindu philosophy practically leads. Illusion being recognised as such, what is more natural than a wish to escape from it? And how succeed in doing this, unless by destroying in one's self all that makes part of this illusive and fugitive world, namely, desire, will, sensation? Meditation has made a void within the soul; there remains to him no further motive of action; he understands that nothing is worth the trouble of a motion, and that he himself does not exist; he seats himself upon his heels and meditates.

Upon what does he meditate? Upon Brahmá. The knowledge of Brahmá is enfranchisement. The Brahma who is one's self, and who perceives himself to be diverse and mutable by the very fact that he recognises himself as Brahma, turns away from the magic mirror of Maya. Let us repeat "I am Brahma," "for he who knows that he is Brahma, is one with Him who is One." Beyond the misty veil of appearances, let us strive to behold Him who is: immediately all barriers of our limited being falling, we become again the eternal and infinite, returning finally into that whence we came forth. It is a singular fact that here, for the first and possibly for the last time, the human being attaches salvation, not to acts, not to faith, not to emotions, not to ceremonies, *but to knowledge*.

"Those whose conduct is good, who read the Vedas and perform the sacrifices, will ascend after death to the abode of the devas, but the fruit of their good works being consumed, they return into this world, for *they are without knowledge*. They are born in new forms, they have will and power and sensation, they live again. This is the worst suffering, and can only be escaped by becoming absorbed into the unconsciousness and inertia of pure Being. The man who sees a difference between Brahma and the world goes from change to change, from death to death." That is to say, he will for ever be reborn.

That a man may enter into calm, he must hold his breath, fix his attention, destroy his senses, cease from speaking. He presses his palate with the tip of the tongue, breathes slowly, looks fixedly at a point in space, and thought ceases, consciousness is abolished, the feeling of personality vanishes.

"We shall cease to feel pleasure and pain, having attained immobility and solitude." The human existence, recognising itself as the absolute Being, is rid of time and space, of number, limit, and quality. "As a spider rising by means of its own thread gains the open space, so he who meditates rises by means of the syllable OM, and gains independence." "That which is without thought, though situated at the heart of all thought;* that which is hid, though at the foundation of all things—let a man plunge his soul into this, and his being will go forth free from its bonds." Thought and will being abolished, the whole phantasmagoria of Maya disappears: "We become like a fire without smoke, or like a traveller, who, having left the carriage which brought him, watches the revolution of its wheels." "Grief can no longer live in us; he who knows Brahma is for ever consoled." That is to say, we comprehend that we are nothing but a spark of the one absolute Being; henceforward, what suffering could reach us? "We no longer say: this body is myself, I am such a person; but *I am Brahma, I am the world.*" "Pure, undeveloped, tranquil, unbreathing, bodiless, eternal, immutable, imperishable, firm, passionless, unborn, independent," I have forever entered into peace, for I have thrown off conscious existence. Such is the supreme felicity, reserved for the adepts of the mysterious doctrine celebrated by the Upanishads with a solemnity of language which gives an idea of the fervour, the enthusiasm, the

* *Cf.* Spinoza.

tremor of restrained hope wherewith the Brahman is thrilled, as he looks forward to that day of deliverance after which he will never again say *Me*, of himself. "He who, knowing the Vedas and having repeated them daily in a consecrated place, having made no creature suffer, concentrates his thoughts upon the Existence, and is absorbed therein, attains the world of Bráhmă, and returns no more ; *no, he returns no more.*"

Thought, cast into a metaphysical vertigo and by its own effort abolishing itself, and the annihilation of the will, are intellectual and moral effects of the Brahmanic philosophy. We see this philosophy emerge from a primitive tendency manifested far back in the Vedic age, and unroll the series of these results. That they are inevitable appears clear, when we observe that elsewhere the same causes have produced the same effects. We cannot consider nations — for the case of India is unique — but we may individuals, for it is surely legitimate to compare the average soul of a race with some individual soul, observing in both the same structure and the same ties. We have had Hindu minds in Europe. In England, where man is so valiant and so active, where personality is so strong and stable, where poetry is so subjective, where religion is a monotheism so Hebraic, Shelley was almost such. Critics have long since noted in him faculties analogous to those which wove the Vedic myths. No poetry is more impersonal, no sympathetic imagination more capable of reproducing the elemental sensations of elemental beings

—the gladness of the earth revolving in the light of space, with its girdle of seas and continents, its forests, its clouds, its humid blue atmosphere; the peace of the splendid cloud floating in the warm ether, then laughing in the thunder and falling in the rain, mother of future harvests; the ecstasy of the lark, intoxicated with the sight of the luminous plains, quivering with joy, throbbing invisible in space,

"Like an unbodied joy whose race has just begun,"

and the timid affection of the fragile plant dreaming of its future buds. Shelley became earth with the earth, a flower with the flower, a brook with the brook, and his poetry is a changeful reflection of changeful nature. He was destitute of that durable emotion on which personality is founded; the sensation of the Me, with him, was reduced to its minimum. He is always speaking of that ecstasy in which the observer becomes one with the object contemplated. His soul is not distinct, isolated in nature, but is all scattered through it. Hence, all natural objects appear to him to be alive and to have a soul; to be capable of sensations; and, moreover, to be constantly in motion, ever changing, always undergoing transformation. The sensation of Life — of Life at the same time one and multiple — this is what his poetry expresses. He recognises a soul of the universe, a soul of which we are the thoughts, into which death absorbs us, which quivers in the worm and in the star; a soul of which nature is the mystic garment, hidden under the things which are seen, and, at rare moments, shining through beautiful and noble forms, as a pale flame within a vase of translucent alabaster. Let a man re-read "Prometheus Unbound," where all beings unite in chorus, and especially that marvellous dialogue of the Earth and the Moon, and let him say if the poet were not intoxicated with that universal, eternally-upspringing life which circulates through all things ; if he were not transported by the vision of the living Brahmá displayed in sounds, and perfumes, and colours. Beyond this, Shelley never went. He never perceived the neuter Bráhmă, motionless, without qualities. Of the two stages of Hindu intelligence and feeling, he passed through the first only. He knew the dream, the gaiety, the ecstasy of the Vedic poets ; he never attained to the inertia of the gymnosophists. A pantheist he was, but with a joyous pantheism, and he remained valiant and sound.

Amiel is a case more nearly complete. He penetrated beneath the living Brahmá, he became benumbed with the torpidity of the "enfranchised" Brahman, and his aptitude for reverie and speculation, the paralysis of his will, had exactly their point of departure in the plastic faculty which we have noted as the origin of the Hindu pantheism. "My mind," he says, "is the empty frame of a thousand effaced images. It is without substance, being now form only. To return into the body has always appeared to me singular, an arbitrary and conventional thing. I appear to myself as a receptacle of phenomena, as a subject without fixed individuality, and hence, resigning myself only with an effort to the rôle of an individual, the inhabitant of a certain city, in a certain country."

From this habitual sensation of seeing in the universe only a misty dream wherein appearances come and go, the distance is short to pessimism and immobility. Hindu inertia, Hindu pessimism, Hindu pantheism, these three stages, of the will, of the emotional nature, and of the intellect, Amiel traversed. He recognises himself as akin to the Brahmans : "This mental phantasmagoria lulls me as it does the Indian yogi; to me, everything is smoke, illusion, vapour, even my own existence. I attach so little importance to all phenomena that they pass over me like gleams of light, and are gone without leaving a trace. Meditation is like opium; it intoxicates, and reduces to transparent vapour the mountains and all that is." This is the hallucination of the solitary Brahman, who, concentrating his thought, sees the procession of the worlds rising like a mist, for thousands of centuries, out of the empty darkness of being. Amiel's reverie embraces the whole world. " Each civilisation," he says, "is like a thousand years' dream, in which heaven and earth, nature and history, *appear* in a phantasmic light, performing a drama invented by the hallucinated soul." He seems to himself no longer a solid substance ; he melts, and becomes a vapour like everything else. "I am fluid as a phantom, which is seen, but cannot be grasped. I resemble a man to the same extent that the manes of Achilles, the shade of Creusa, were like human beings. Without having died, I am a ghost. Others appear to me as a dream; I am a dream to others." Such is the strange sensation which, repeated upon successive generations, has produced not only Hindu philosophy, but many of the characteristics of Hindu civilisation. Observe that there is not a fact noted in these two volumes of Amiel's "Confessions," not a detail of real life. Naturally, when one is devoted to the contemplation of the infinite, and occupies himself with the absolute, how should he be interested in the accidental and the limited? When the whole world seems a vapoury illusion, why should a man care to study it, in the view of finding for himself the best place there? The solid foundation upon which we rest our seventy years of human life disappears all at once, and the individual, losing his interest in the real and visible world, loses also his hold upon it.

This is the case in India. With the exception of philosophy and astronomy, which treat of what is eternal, the Hindus have had no sciences. They have not had, as the Greeks had, the curiosity to seek out the laws which govern facts; they have not enlightened their obscure vision of nature. Certain of the Upanishads seem written by children or insane persons. Dogs and flamingos converse and philosophise. There is no history. This abundant literature is all reverie and metaphysics. Not a date, not an anecdote, not a serious genealogy. Almost all that we know of the greatest religious event of Asia reaches us through the accounts given by Chinese pilgrims. Of Buddhism we are told neither when it begins, nor how and when it disappears from India. But what more foolish than to study social conditions, civilisations, the history of mankind, if mankind, society, civilisation, are, as Amiel says, only dreams projected by the soul, only waves rising for an instant on the surface of Brahma! As a matter of fact, there is here no effort at social organisation, no precise grouping in states or nations, no constitution definite and secure. Once Brahmanism is established, and the philosophic dream begun, there is no resistance to attacks from without. Her civil, military, and political organisation being rudimentary, India, incapable of definite form, is gelatinous, so to speak; vague, incoherent, powerless, at the mercy of the first aggressive comer, Musalman or English, what does it matter to her, provided only she is left to her dream of that which is durable, that which truly *is*, a knowledge of which enfranchises from sorrow; provided only that she is permitted to intoxicate herself with Being, in the repetition of the syllable OM which gives peace!

December 2.

This morning I return to the river bank. To understand Brahmanic India, no spectacle is so useful as a sight of this people in their out-of-door life on the bank of the sacred Ganges. Here they pray, they loiter, they converse, they eat, they fall asleep, they die. Upon litters the sick and the dying lie extended, some of them brought from great distances to end here. Even the form that was once a living being is destroyed in the presence of the river; for here is the place of cremation. There are the funeral piles, and near them the unconcerned crowd continues splashing in the river, praying, drawing water, performing its ablutions. A few steps distant from the sad spot, men turn their backs to it, and dry themselves calmly, sitting in the sun. Like a natural and familiar occurrence, the dissolution of the individual goes on amid the general life of which it is but an incident. There is nothing frightful about it. Certainly, to the Hindu, the Me has not that strength of coherence which makes us believe in its inevitable permanency, which gives to us will to live, and will not let us think without horror of annihilation. After a body has been burned, the relatives do not weep, but sing: "Is it not folly to wish anything lasting in man? Is he not fleeting as a bubble on the water, frail as the stem of a flower? Earth, ocean, and the gods must perish. Why, then, should not the world of men, evanescent as foam, be seized by universal death, and perish also?"

I watched it take place, this disappearance of a human form. A Brahman presides over the cremations, ensconced in a dark rectangular niche at the top of a small square tower, impassive, a cap on his head, the meagreness of his body visible through his yellow garment. At the foot of the tower are heaps of wood, and here and there, as if thrown down carelessly, tightly strapped in pink or purple coverings, secured within four green bamboos, lie rigid figures. Two fires are burning: on one the corpse is still intact, the limbs secured with cords as if trussed for the spit; the other pile has just ceased blazing, and tiny rose-coloured flames are quivering over the ashes and charred wood and calcined bones. Then the horrible heap is thrown into the Ganges, and floats slowly away on the tranquil current. The brown stain broadens, then disappears, on the smooth surface of the heavy water. All around there is a vague dazzle of colour in a mist of light, a confused rustling, and the splendid flight of screaming birds.

Every day this scene is repeated. There is noisy music of gongs when an old man is burned; but if the person is very young there is wailing, and a mourning procession walks round the pyre.

Between the palaces which crown the *ghats*, the flights of stairs ascend—broad at the water's edge, and growing narrower till they vanish under dark doorways. On the steps, women, statuesque in their blue draperies, very upright, support grandly with lifted arms the vessels full of river water, the heavy copper jars that they carry on their heads. Others carry baskets full of white flowers, and place them in front of tranquil cows.

I make my way upward through narrow lanes, full of white light, where the shadows are sharply outlined on the pavements. On the walls blue elephants are marching up, loaded with gods. At the corners of the houses are altars or little temples, where the ceremonial flowers are in heaps before grotesque images. Through windows somewhat of the indoor life can be seen; always the same low square rooms with their range of colonnettes; dark courtyards, sculptured walls. Around us there are more and more monsters and chapels, crowded and heaped one upon another; there is an orgy of sacred figures, shrines, altars, in the tortuous lane. The white eyeballs of gods gleam in the shadow, their multiplied arms writhe, their mouths grimace frightfully. This one is Mahakal, or the Great Fate; this is the god Bhaironath, chief policeman, who keeps order in Benares, and his club is also a divinity, represented by a stone covered with a mask; this is the genius of the planet Saturn, whose silver head emerges from a platform; this is Anupurna, "the good goddess," who feeds all her worshippers; and here, as everywhere else, is the son of Siva, the astonishing Ganesa, seated, his legs crossed, his stout waist girt with the Brahman's sacred cord, and his red elephant's trunk lying on the ground in voluminous folds; while, at the feet of the huge clumsy divinity, is the tiny mouse, bridled and saddled, which serves him as a courser. Across gratings I catch a rapid glimpse of a Brahman seated on the ground before the idol whose guardian he is, his eyes fixed, his meagre limbs motionless. In dark corners are sacred wells, into which the crowd throw flowers—the well of Fate, that of Science, that of Mankarnika.

As we advance, it is with difficulty that we force

our way through the crowd. The narrow lanes are made still narrower by projecting stalls where there are masses of rosaries and statuettes, and, especially, great yellow heaps of jasmine. The air is thick with the odour from all these people, these flowers, and these wells of stagnant water; we make our way onward through the noise of prayers, confused, elbowed, crowded, carried by the multitude, pushed against by a hundred screaming beggars; and always there are rows of idols, and chapels whose porches are guarded by motionless fakirs. Finally an odour more nauseating, [of fetid mud as from a cow-yard, together with decomposed flowers, announces the great temple of Siva. Here is its gilded dome, here are its towers, not isolated in an open space, but crowded close by houses, encroached upon by shops, rising in the very heart of these lanes. This is the centre of the Hindu ant-hill; and, like an ant-hill, it is in feverish, disorderly agitation. There is no common action on the part of this multitude; each is going his own way, regardless of every one else. Old women of Brahmanic race, white-faced, in their white draperies, toothless, stumbling, muttering, go by like sleep-walkers; with hysterical gestures they throw flowers upon the ground, or sprinkle it with Ganges water. In the presence of all this multitude, priests, with sanctimonious air, sit drowsing in the sun, at the entrance of the temple. There are men running rapidly around two trees; there are others calling upon Siva, and striking bells hung in a row before his sanctuaries. There are files of trembling old Brahmans, grey-haired and ill-shaven, who, leaning against each other, advance with difficulty; there are mendicants with white skin, of a wan white, entirely white hair, and a sort of collar of greyish beard. Many faces quite European catch your eye for a moment, then are lost in the crowd. You recognise very rapidly the fellow-Aryan, the man of our own race, but brutalised or enfeebled in mind by successive invasions, by tyrannies, by the burning climate, by centuries of suffering. The look is strange, fevered, or idiotic. There is an air of insanity everywhere.

Within the temple, on the black pavement, slippery with mud and the crushed flowers, this eddy of the human tide carries us at random, under colonnades, past infected wells, where men, leaning over, are anxiously seeking to see their own image in the water; past a colossal statue of a bull in red stone, into a sacred cow-house, where the animals, their mouths filled with flowers, their eyes shut, regally accept the worship of the insane multitude; and, suddenly, a shiver of terror—I have brushed against an indescribable object, a naked creature of uniform grey colour, rigid as stone—a fakir, covered with ashes, who seems to be dead, and does not even start at the collision; and now, hustled by the crowd, suffocated, terrified, I find myself, without any idea how, again among the little lanes where the flowers are sold. From here I see the human wave flowing slow, a dense crowd around the pagoda. The portico is guarded by mendicant Brahmans, old bald-heads nodding with stupor. Above them, the painted image of the lord of Benares, the ascetic god, Siva, who creates and destroys, emblem of the Power which reproduces all beings, and, from millions of deaths, calls forth millions of lives.

December 3.

After a few days passed in this Hindu world, the mind begins to be filled with Hindu impressions. To-day, in leaving the temple of Siva, it seemed to me that, under these diverse images, I begin to make out a fundamental idea, as, in the different notes of a musical instrument, you recognise the same *timbre*.

Observe this vase of Benares brass. You admire the lustre of the metal, the fineness of the chasing ; but these are only peculiarities of brass vases. Observe another characteristic more interesting, because very general : what does all this chasing represent ? At first sight, you scarcely know ; it seems only a confusion of lines, curving, interlaced, entangled by chance. By degrees, vague forms are discernible—gods, genii, fish, dogs, gazelles, flowers, grass ; not grouped after any design, but thrown together, piled one over another in a confused living heap, like the slimy mass brought up in a net, where, amid the seaweed, you can discern claws that move, scales that glitter, and the twisting and writhing of soft creatures. So, every one of these chasings is endlessly complicated ; these gods have their six arms ; these plants extend in every direction with stems and leaves; these flowers are entwined and twisted into each other. In short, nothing is simple; everything is multiple, tufty, and this complexity, for want of leading lines, remains irregular.

Accumulated *number*, without order or proportion, is the characteristic to be discovered here at every moment: in this inundation of divinities who overflow their temples and fill all the streets with their multitude; in this ant-hill of men of every colour and caste, which rustles in the morning on the river bank; in this human wave which just now swept around the images of Siva; in this confusion of chapels, altars, sacred wells, statues of animals; not forming simple, geometrical figures,— as in ancient Egypt, where avenues of sphinxes, ending in pyramidal pylons, gave access to rectangular courts, — but scattered at random, in tortuous lanes, amid shops and houses. This characteristic appears, again, in the strange architectural constructions, where stone grows out of stone, as a leaf out of a leaf; and torsos, heads, arms, legs of gods innumerable, bodies of quadrupeds and of snakes abound, crushing each other, rising in a confused pyramid of living forms. Spontaneously, owing to a special construction of the Hindu mind, things appear to these people as infinitely complex. While the Greek was especially sensible of the correct and the well-ordered, the Hindu perceives chiefly the multitudinous and the diverse. External nature does not seem to him a harmonious and limited whole, but rather an immense vegetation, with ever-increasing branches, an inextricable network of offshoots, all growing vigorously and unrestrained.

To understand the Hindu point of view, contrast it with our theistic position. These people of India never conceived of an intelligent and moral architect of the universe, who made man in his own image, by intelligence and reason, sovereign of the creation which, in perfect order, in classes and species and genera, lay below him. They do not feel themselves separated from creation, but brothers of all living things, making part of Nature, born of her, and yet oppressed and crushed by her grandeur and multiplicity. They fix no date of six thousand years ago for the beginning of things. Consider those gigantic poems, those endless enumerations, those prodigious accumulations of figures, those myriads of millions of centuries, those frantic metaphors prolonged beyond all possibility of the mind's following them, by which Hindu authors strive to figure the immensity of the universe, the infinity of space and time; and you will perceive that they have had, carried almost to vertigo, the sensation of the illimitable; not an abstract, mathematical infinity, which can be expressed by a symbol, but the living illimitable, wherein grow, unite, contend, all forms and all forces, and to symbolise which all their work, in its extravagance and disorder, aims.

The present religion of India is a Hindu work, as complicated, irregular, and multitudinous as a pagoda-roof or the chasing of a Benares vase. It was developed out of Brahmanism, as leaves, flowers, seed, grow out of a straight and simple stem. First, say the old Brahmans, there is one ; then he becomes three ; then five, then seven, then nine ; then they say he is eleven, and a hundred and ten, and a thousand and twenty. It is these thousand and twenty forms of Being, that is to say, the infinite variety of these forms, which Hinduism adores. As they are of every kind, vague and diverse, so the religion will be diverse and vague. Its sects, its rites, its divinities, its doctrines are innumerable. It is impossible to grasp it, to discover its dogmas and fundamental articles of faith, to disentangle its great general outlines. There is everything in Hinduism. Take all the beliefs of the human race, all the religious observances which express these beliefs, Christianity, Islamism, Buddhism, ancient polytheism, fetichism ; the worship of the forces of nature, the worship of ancestors, of demons, of the sparrow-hawk, of animals; plunge all this into a philosophic pantheism, and you will have that extraordinary whole, made up of contradictions and incoherences, which is called Hinduism.

The Brahman who, concentrating his thought, strives to lose himself in Brahma ; this inert fakir who, with arms stretched for years toward the sky, aspires to the paradise of Siva ; this rajah who, in honour of Vishnu, the charitable god, devotes three hundred rupees daily for the support of the poor ; this Saktist, who plunges into mystic orgies ; this Sudra, kneeling before a round stone — these all are members of the great religious community of India. Between the different sects there is no profound separation. The worshipper of Siva calls the worshipper of Vishnu a brother. Not that he sees in Vishnu a second divinity, equal or inferior to Siva, but that he considers Vishnu as also manifesting Siva, as himself contained in Siva. Each god is so varied in his forms and his attributes that, in certain forms and certain attributes common to all, they all meet and blend. Siva, who is lord of death, is also lord of life. He is love, and terror ; harmful, and benignant ; he is the great ascetic ; he is a scholar and a philosopher ; he is a mountaineer, merry and wild ; a Bacchus, drunken and dancing, followed by a troop of intoxicated buffoons. His images express the diversity of these attributes ; he has five faces, six arms, three eyes, a thousand and eight names. Hence, his cult is within the reach of all. The Hindu professor who was my guide yesterday in the University bore on his forehead the three horizontal lines of the Sivaists. Probably he adores in Siva, "the producer and the destroyer"; that is to say, the eternal activity of Being which, unfolding itself with this double rhythm, organising and dissolving all beings, may be simply a supreme God, personal and creative. On the other hand, when the black worshipper expels demons by covering his cabin with the excrement with which Siva's bull has furnished him ; when he sprinkles the stone which symbolises the god ; when he rings a bell to awaken it ; when he dresses this stone ; when he covers it with food, — with cream, with curry, with rice, with cakes, — when he deluges it with perfumes, he practises only the savage cult of the stone and the bull.

Nor have they any system of morals, anterior to religion and of higher range, that is present to guide in any one direction the mass of beliefs and ceremonials. The orgies of certain sects and the self-torture of the fakirs are two forms of the cult of Siva. It matters not that they are mutually contradictory; the series of sacred texts extends over a period of time so long, they were composed at periods so different in the social development, they form a mass so enormous, that they authorise all morals and all dogmas, and the religion of each sect forms a system as vague, as inconsistent, as the Hindu religion in its entire mass.

For instance, what is Vishnuism? Originally, Vishnu is "the preserver." Between Siva who organises and Siva who dissolves there is a space for a power that supports. This plant, which has sprung out of the soil, will presently return into the soil; meanwhile, by the effect of an interior force, it lives and retains its form. This force, which thus sustains the entire world, is Vishnu, whose ordinary symbol is very appropriately a tree. Becoming popular, the abstraction becomes also a distinct being, a personal divinity, without whose aid the world would perish; hence, a divinity who is charitable and kind, and, in ten successive incarnations,—as a fish, a tortoise, a wild boar, a lion, a dwarf, Rama, Krishna, Buddha,—has come into the world for its salvation.

Thus multiplied and developed, Vishnu disappears, as a stem is concealed by its own vegetation; and nothing further is seen of him but his incarnations. Two of these, Rama and Krishna, are especially popular, and the cult and doctrines of their worshippers go on changing and multiplying, extending their ramifications through the centuries. Sects produce other sects; and, around the central stem, such a mass of them have budded forth that only this confused mass can be perceived. In the eleventh century, in the twelfth and thirteenth, twice in the fifteenth, again in the sixteenth and eighteenth, and once more, very recently, religious leaders have arisen who have added to the extension of Vishnuism. Some of these teachers, pantheists, recognise only one substance in divers manifestations; others distinguish two irreducible principles. Madhava accepts all the gods, but subordinates them to Vishnu, who alone is immortal. Some do not concern themselves with metaphysical speculations. They make no address to the intellect; they appeal only to the heart. One thing only is important, faith in Krishna, who has loved mankind; and, with this, goodwill and love to our brethren, all living creatures. Besides these teachers, who are the greatest, there is an infinity of others. As soon as, amid the suffering multitude, there stands up a man as a messenger of God, he finds disciples; a sect gathers around him. Meanwhile legends grow and multiply; a thousand rude images translate to the ignorant masses the fervent ideas of an inspired few. In turn, these men are venerated as gods, as partial incarnations of divinity. It is singular that, instead of being mutually hostile or destructive, these different beliefs add themselves to one another, subsist together upon the trunk of Vishnuism, as last spring's offshoot grows beside the older branches. A doctrine of the eleventh century will have adepts who live as brethren with the disciples of a master not fifty years dead. Like a living thing, the religion of Vishnu retains all the forms through which it has passed, all the scions which it has thrown out in the different centuries. Like a living thing, also, it contains in itself the principle of its development, while it draws material from its environment. The idolatry of the black races, Buddhism, the religions of Islam, Christianity, have in their turn furnished elements which it has assimilated.

To-day, destitute of precise dogma, of regular hierarchy, formed by a hundred groups living one beside another, it suggests those primitive organisms, those pulpy creatures with tentacles innumerable, destitute of vertebræ or bony system, capable of resisting any mutilation exactly because they are composed of independent centres, of which each could be wounded to death without the destruction of the whole. Such is also Hinduism, of which this religion of Vishnu, so varied and so comprehensive, is nevertheless but a part. At Calcutta, an Englishman was expressing in my presence his regret at the meagre success of the Protestant missions. A few Hindus are converted, frequently from interested motives, to obtain employment from Europeans. After some years they return into their caste and their sect. The Brahmans listen with patience, toleration, and curiosity. Their own religion is a thing too fugitive and multiple to be encountered hand to hand. It cannot be refuted, as English missionaries seek to refute the Muhammadan faith. Instead of being destroyed or arrested by the obstacle which the apostles of Christianity oppose to it, so powerful is the vitality of Hinduism, so great its adaptive faculty, that it surrounds, envelops, absorbs the obstacle; and pursues its growth, enriched by a new philosophic and religious idea. Thus the Brahman teachers offer to receive the Christ among the three hundred and thirty million divinities of the Hindu pantheon, provided it be permitted them to consider him as one of the forms of Vishnu, incarnated for Europeans. Thus, at Calcutta, the new sect, the Brahmo-Somaj, adopts the moral theism of English liberal Christianity. The existence of a personal God, eternal, distinct from creation; the paternal government of the world; the distinction of soul and body; future rewards and punishments—all these general ideas of that moderate and reasonable philosophy now current in England, this sect freely adopts. In the same way, formerly, Hinduism, not rejecting, but only eliminating slowly the dogmatic elements of Buddhism, fed upon its substance. Gentleness, universal kindness, extended even to animals, asceticism—by all these traits the soul of Sakya-Muni still inhabits the peninsula.

Thus lives and grows the religion of India, the most plastic of all religions, the most capable of adapting itself to circumstances; so complex, made up of elements so dissimilar and changeful, so uncertain in form and direction, that it does not seem to be a religion; and still it may be called such, as we give the name of *India* to this geographic whole, made of countries and climates so diverse; as we call *Hindu* this human group where are mingled races of all colours and all stages of civilisation, and yet, not without a certain unity. At first, clear, at its pantheistic source; then made obscure by the religious ideas of conquered and conquering peoples; extended over thirty centuries, of which each one has modified its form and added to its contents; to-day the Hindu religion is spread out as an immense network of beliefs, observances, morals, philosophies, sects, in which the eye no longer can recognise any general outlines. So the Ganges, broad and turbid, swollen with the incessant afflux of tributary rivers, loaded with vegetable débris as it flows through jungles, through ancient cities, through English cities, overflows its banks, spreading out in undefined sheets, covers great extents of country with its milky water, then slackens its current, deposits its mud and fertilising slime; and thus extending its length and its undefined delta, divides, ramifies, is lost in a thousand obscure and tortuous mouths.

Half seen, half guessed at in its great features, I leave this religious world of India. This evening I bid adieu to great Benares, and I have come once more to the sacred shore of the old Ganges, where, for the first time, in the morning light, I felt the rustling, palpitating life of this ancient race of mankind.

I have sent my guide away, and wander along the bank alone. The crowd is gone from the palaces and the great pyramidal stairs. I hear the little sound of the water against the marble— the quivering water, on whose surface a faint rose-colour still trembles, which now dies, giving place to pale lights, wan gleams. In the peaceful atmosphere of evening, things come out clearer and more solid than in the glitter of the day. Opposite me, across the great slow river, there is the pallid stretch of barren sands. Between the desert and the lofty pagan edifices the Ganges describes its gradual curve.

I wander at random over the pavements, among the blocks of a ruined temple, between red columns, in front of imposing palaces. The last women coming up from the river, laden with their water-jars, pass, slow and stately. Great lean dogs lie stretched out on the steps; and here and there between the chapels of pink granite, the cow, a living idol, reposes from the day's adoration. A few Brahmans, their followers all gone, remain solitary, seated upon their stone tables; two of them are murmuring with modulations as of a plain-chant, the last prayers of the evening; three others are silent in the presence of the grey water —the grey water, rippling and flowing eternally.

And now, above, from a terrace resound deep, heavy strokes of a gong, whose vibration strikes through me, and then the solitary voice of a trumpet arises, nasal and strident, in the vast silence— minor scales, simplified and rapid, with the sharp *timbre* of a bagpipe— plaintive notes, prolonged, repeated with insistence, like a grief that one cannot leave alone; unexpected modulations, almost discords, which disturb and torment; a peculiar rhythm, a Hindu music, made for the soul of a different humanity, so sad in its very strangeness, that, without comprehending it, one shivers at the sound.

Darkness has invaded all the space; the long row of temples has disappeared into the night. The three Brahmans are still there, seated on their heels, their heads bent toward the dark water.

And still I hear this bagpipe voice.

CHAPTER VI

LUCKNOW   CAWNPUR   AGRA

December 6.

THIS India is very varied. At seventy leagues from Benares, the great pagan city, begins another world. Lucknow is a Muhammadan and English city. Sumptuous hotels, elegant white villas in their luxuriant grounds, broad avenues, vast, well-kept parks where trot well-appointed riders, companies of Scots Greys, with blond soldierly faces, factory chimneys smoking on the horizon—these are what I have already seen in Calcutta. The Saracenic architecture of the mosques is beautiful and simple, tranquillising after the Hindu frenzies. But the material is poor; the buildings are plaster, for which reason one has no desire to see them again.

The most beautiful thing here is nature, happy and peaceful, not lawless and oppressive, as in the humid South. The sky is of a pale blue; the air is stirred with a light breeze that is almost cool; instead of endless tall palms, there are slender trees with delicate rustling foliage. Oranges and mandarins shine golden in the groves; and great fragile roses, more splendid than ours, spread a familiar perfume. Such must be Persian nature, in the poems of Firdausi.

There is the same tranquil beauty, the same happy blossoming of flowers, in the cemetery of Lucknow where lie the dead of 1857. The Residence, which Sir Henry Lawrence with his handful of soldiers so long defended, is a heap of ruins, blackened by fire, torn by cannon-shot, all covered now with the green of climbing plants, where flame great drooping clusters of yellow flowers.

I have been re-reading the story of the siege. What impresses one in this narrative is the sentiment that supported the defenders. There was something besides courage and love of country or desire of glory; I mean, first, a certain grave pride and tenacity; and then, a religious sentiment very serious and very lofty. Every morning the officers and soldiers, with the women and children who had been brought into the Residence for shelter, sang psalms—those which their persecuted Puritan ancestors had sung to strengthen their courage and support them; and the grand Biblical verses gave them that grave and silent enthusiasm, that fervour, which makes men able calmly and coolly to sacrifice their lives. "Here lies Henry Lawrence, who tried to do his duty. May the Lord have mercy upon his soul!" says a slab in the little fragrant cemetery.

To-day, in Cawnpur, I have seen the well into which Nana Sahib flung the still palpitating bodies of the women and children massacred at his command. All around it is now the silence of a great park, and the calm of flowers. A marble angel with folded wings stands on the edge of the well, which has been surrounded with a Gothic balustrade. The downcast eyes have a divine serenity, the clasped hands droop with a gesture of forgiveness.

December 7.

We are on our way toward the Musalman country, going straight to the North-west. I much admire the Indian railways. In the *cabinets de toilette* you can have a douche; there are little beds that can be pulled down if you wish to recline; and, by night, every traveller of first or second class has a right to one of these little beds. If you wish to have your meals on the road, you notify the conductor, who orders them by telegraph, and the table is ready at the stations where the train stops, in the morning, for breakfast; at one o'clock, for tiffin; at six, for dinner. Thus you traverse, without fatigue, distances of a thousand miles; and you think with pity of those poor travellers who, leaving Paris by evening train, reach Marseilles or Brest, tired to death, and feverish with the sleepless night.

Among my travelling companions I observe always the same friendly and social disposition. Officers, missionaries, business men—in fifteen minutes you have made the acquaintance of them all, and there is the courteous conversation of gentlemen, almost always instructive. They are interested in public affairs, they have ideas as to the future of India, as to the progress of Russia. One of them said to me that in fifty years India would have its autonomous parliament. He is an advocate of this. "Our duty," he says, "is the education of India." Observe, to make an Englishwoman of *her*—the old Asiatic queen! "When this education is completed, we shall have nothing further to do but to withdraw. We shall have done our duty by India." His daughters listened, two charming English girls, all fresh and pink, in their simple gowns of light flannel. The calmness and gravity of their faces were striking. These are not adventurers, these English colonists, but honest, energetic fathers of families, who live in all the peace and happiness of an English home.

"England is doing her duty toward India;" she is civilising India. For instance, to destroy caste prejudices, she is employing a very effectual method: she makes the Hindus travel. By traversing different regions of the peninsula, by elbowing each other in railway trains, they learn much, and their minds must needs be enlarged. For this reason the railway companies keep their prices as low as possible. The ticket on which my "boy" travels three thousand miles, from Calcutta to Calcutta, by Delhi and Bombay, costs forty-four rupees (twenty-two dollars). Consequently, the third-class carriages are always crowded with Hindus, a motley and picturesque load.

This line, constructed and owned by an English company, is worked by the native people. Hindu are the engineers, Hindu the conductors and the

L

stationmasters, which is at once apparent by the way the service is carried on. There is none of the automatic precision, the calm exactitude, the gravity and determination of English employés. At Benares I desired to send my luggage at once to Bombay. Thereupon the station was thrown into confusion; there were colloquies between the stationmaster and the various clerks and ticket-sellers, and my "boy"; colloquies quite undignified, abounding in gestures and outcries, a great flux of words. We were twenty minutes belated in starting, and I had been obliged myself to paste the labels on my boxes. No, India is not yet altogether anglicised; no, her "education" is not yet complete.

At the stations my "boy" gets down quickly from his carriage to see if I desire fruit. He is forty-eight years old, short, thin, puny, a real Bengali, delicate and sickly. Very precious, this "boy"—at once a guide, servant, interpreter, and companion. Only it is understood that he is not to serve at table. To see a Christian hog eating, to inhale the odour of meats—this would be a pollution not to be thought of. As he knows the English language well, and is familiar with the country we traverse, he requires thirty rupees a month; on this he feeds himself, very frugally, it is true: a little rice, which he boils in his brass jar, and eats sitting on his heels on the ground; and a little water to wash his mouth, according to ceremonial: he requires nothing more. His duty is to have the luggage registered, to know the number of my packages, to be perpetually counting them, to see that nothing is lost. Not a handkerchief can go astray but in three minutes he knows it, and obliges me to rummage in all my pockets. Hindu by race and by religion, in sect a Sivaist, he seems particularly to venerate cows and monkeys. When once I endeavoured to rally him on this subject he smiled mysteriously, but would not speak.

Cheddy belongs to the Sudra caste, which was created from the feet of Brahma, we are told: " Pure, in body and mind, the humble servitor of the higher classes, gentle of speech, never arrogant, seeking shelter with the Brahmans," such is, says Manu, the true Sudra. This one, who is about as stout and strong as a grasshopper, would sink under the weight of a satchel; and it is agreed that he shall carry nothing. To make amends, he follows me like my shadow, sleeping across my threshold like a little faithful dog, and fights like a lion with the beggars who assail me. He knows a few words of Sanskrit, also English, Bengali, Hindustani, and the history of the rajahs, the shahs, and the khans; and in the evening, by the light of a lantern, seated outside my door, he reads in some mysterious volume. But notwithstanding all this knowledge, his heart is humble, a truly timid and pure Sudra's heart.

We converse. Although a pupil of Protestant missionaries in Calcutta, he is not a convert. He is very fond of the English : "English judge says to poor man, 'You are right;' and to rich man,

'You are wrong!'" Here we have the little fact which, often repeated, secures English rule in India. Under this *régime* the peasant is unmolested. He is no longer hunted down and harassed by all the functionaries of the native or Musalman governments: he pays a small regular tax, and he is master of his earnings. He has a feeling entirely new to the Hindu peasant, that of security.

On the other hand, Cheddy Lal does not love the British soldier. "Too proud," he says to me; "poor Hindu carry all their luggage." This single sentence suffices. You see the arrogance, the haughty silence of him, of Tommy Atkins realising in India the dream of the English lower classes to treat himself as "a gentleman," and have himself waited on. How often have I seen him as he steps from a train, proud and calm, his head held high, his fair hair well pomatumed, correctly gloved, switch in hand, making his spurs clink, and with his lofty, big-chested stature dominating the crowd of coolies who stagger under the weight of his travelling-bags!

Ever toward the North-west we run, toward the land of the Musalman. The country is beautiful: interminable, solitary plains, all silvery with the white shiver of tall reeds. To the horizon's edge they crowd, one upon another, lifting out of its sheath a tall dry stem, at whose summit trembles a plume pale and light as smoke. Sometimes antelopes come in sight at a little trot, then stop and look, one foot held up, the slender head turned anxiously toward us. Storks and herons, very serious, watch us as we pass. The great sky is vaporous with light; before us the rails stretch in shining, rigid lines, meeting in the distance, at a point that we shall never reach! By night, the darkness and solitude in these desolate plains are solemn, and now and then an almost imperceptible cry, guessed at in the great silence, the far-off yelp of a jackal, is vaguely sad.

December 9.

I am in the capital of the ancient Moguls; and there are many things to see, especially in architecture, palaces, and tombs. For they struggled against time and death, these Musalmans. They did not accept being totally abolished. While the peaceful and meditative Hindu returned without a struggle, without leaving any trace behind him, into the bosom of that being which, for an instant, had thrown him out upon the surface of this illusory world—they, the passionate and self-willed, asserted themselves after death in jasper and marble, as they had impressed themselves, during their lives, with fire and sword.

Akbar was one of these; and his tomb stands, intact as on its first day, in the silent country. Four great gates, facing toward the four cardinal points, four triumphal arches, flanked with minarets, crowned with bell-towers, give access to a solitary garden, where golden fruit hangs amid the foliage. From each gate leads a broad road with red pavement, and all converge toward the central monument. It is at once Chinese and Saracenic, this tomb, consisting of a succession of terraces, retreating as they rise, surmounted by Mongol kiosks. Here the solid rests upon the open : upon rows of colonnettes rise marble walls incrusted with precious stones, which are set with absolute regularity, and blaze upon the perfect white of the surface. Each terrace is a quadrilateral, paved with mosaic, framed in its slender columns, connected with each other by Saracenic arches. Behind these marble columns a corridor surrounds the terrace, closed on the outer side by a lace of white stone, exquisitely relieved against the pale blue of the sky. Light and delicate as it is, this architecture of perfect stone seems indestructible in this youthful, luminous atmosphere which penetrates it from every side.

Within the centre of the building, at the mathematical point where the diagonals of the square intersect, is the great tomb of Akbar, a rectangle of marble, on whose surface are only a few lotus flowers in relief, the frail stems creeping over it very timidly and gently. There in the shadow the Mogul has been sleeping for two hundred years. Outside, to glorify him in the light, there are the graceful curves of the carved marble, the splendour of the coloured paving-stones, the profusion of mosaics, the purity of perfect lines, the consummate art which cost the labour of an uncounted multitude of workmen. They are all dead; but this perfect architectural work, one of the noblest achievements of their race, stands here under the sky in the peaceful country.

There are sounds of accordions floating in the air. Some English soldiers, lounging on the terrace, are playing their national airs. Leaning upon this exquisite balustrade, four of them are smoking their briarwood pipes; and the smoke curls upward, tranquil and calm, like the rest of the scene.

It is good to note with accuracy the details of a vision that one will never see again. To-day, the 9th of December, at half-past eleven, this is what I have under my eyes, from the summit of the tomb of Akbar. Outside of the lacework of stone and the white kiosks that bound it, lies a vast square carpet, the great park, with its dense clumps of trees and the brilliancy of its flowers, girt with a bastioned wall. To the north, south, east, and west, fifteen hundred feet away from the tomb, are the four imposing gates, four angular surfaces of red granite, brightened with white marble, each with its immense Moorish archway. Beyond, in every direction, lies the great tawny plain. Domes of trees make spots of verdure upon the withered, yellow grass. On the east there are ribbons of blue water. Here and there, in the desolate country, columns and towers rise among the shrubs and trees, the ruins of a city which has left only these few imperishable monuments; and, standing quite by itself, the pale splendour of the marbles of the Taj, bluish in the misty light, like heaps of distant snow.

At the citadel.—A curious fortress of red sandstone on the shore of the Jumna. On the summit of the rugged walls and massive bastions, made to resist assaults and rising like cliffs out of the river, there runs the most delicate embroidery of faintly-tinted marble, rendered more exquisite by contrast with the huge rough masonry on which it rests. It is a rock crowned with lacework, in which cannon - balls have made pitiful rents. In the fortress there is everything—mosques, harems, palaces, halls of justice, gardens, a whole marble city, hidden behind the lofty crenellated walls, a whole royal city, or rather, it is an entire camp,* whose chief, sheltered behind the thickness of the accumulated stone, surrounded by his ministers, his counsellors, his generals, his poets, his musicians, his wives, fulfilled his duties as emperor and Musalman, enjoying, meanwhile, the refined delights, the consummate luxury, of an artistic and amorous tyrant.

Crossing a drawbridge, passing under a fortified gateway and in front of a guard-house, past lounging European soldiers, one comes to a broad paved road, which rises between the bastions and gives access to the interior, where edifices are crowded together like the tents in a camp.

First, the Moti-Masjid. Around the three sides of a square court with marble pavement, stands the marble mosque. Fifty-eight stout columns, united by Saracenic arches, carved in floral designs, support the heavy flat roof, and in this deep gallery the marble has the soft, warm tints

---

* The forts of Delhi and Agra are permanent camps copied from the Mongol camps of the steppes.

of old ivory. There is nothing more, neither painting nor woodwork—two colours only, the blue of the sky, the white of the marble; and this sumptuous simplicity, this splendour of sunlight on the pure stone, express better than anything else could the spiritual ardour, the enthusiasm of the Musalman soul.

Upon the roof, three pointed domes expand their glittering balls, outline their admirable curves against a pale sky, which is so light, so pure, that it seems devoid of air, a mere ether containing nothing but light.

Then there is a succession of great courtyards, closed on three sides: the Court of Tournaments, where horses pranced, and tigers and elephants fought in the presence of the emperor; the Diwan-i-Khas, where, from his throne of black marble, Akbar pronounced his sentences of death; the Diwan-y-Am; the Jahangir Mahal; then corridors whose walls are incrusted with birds and flowers,— parrots of emeralds, lotus flowers of lapis-lazuli,— whose windows are made of a single slab of marble cut out in open-work. And with all this wealth of display, these incrustations of gems, the outlines and tones and lights are harmonious; all is simple and perfectly proportioned, as in a Greek temple. This was a spontaneous efflorescence of art, perfect like that of the free cities of Hellas, testifying to a no less refined education of taste and intellect, reaching its climax under religious despots who, masters of the lives and of the labour of a great people, crushed and kneaded the human material, that they might render eternal their own vision of beauty.

What modern poet has ever had a dream so delicious as that Mogul who built the *zenanas* and the women's bathrooms? In rooms to which the daylight has no access, cool with the coolness of marble, there are great basins of jade, the running water dripping from one to another of them. Upon the translucent white of the walls and columns, ten thousand little facetted mirrors gleam like diamonds in the darkness, and reflect the light of innumerable tiny lamps burning in niches. The "Thousand and One Nights" has conceived no such vision; it is a palace of fairies or genii, situated underground, far from our world, remote from sunlight, built of precious stones, full of darkness, yet lighted up by the inner fire of these gems.

Within, imagine what Akbar used to see—the graceful crowd of Circassian and Arab, and Hindu women, the pick of all Asia chosen by a tyrant's caprice; the indolent girls, lying along a basin's edge, dipping a bare foot in the water; the sleepy girls, lulled by the cool murmur of running streamlets; girls bathing, wringing their heavy, wet hair, reflected in the shadowy, liquid mirror; and the whole wrapped in a vague, mysterious light: verily, for Akbar, after affairs of state, in the oppressive heat of noonday, this was a cool, peaceful, delicious place.

In the upper part of the fortress, separated by gardens from the emperor's palace, on a terrace overhanging the river and commanding a view of the whole plain, is the women's apartment—six chambers of spotless marble, whose walls, of open fretwork, or simply with rectangles here and there cut out, allow free passage to light and air. This harem is the dainty pearl crowning the red bastions of the fortress. Literally, these dwelling-places are made of precious stones; all the walls are jewels. Over the twelve sides of each of the slender columns creep delicate, twining stems, whose flowers are amethysts and turquoises. Along the marble walls, other flowers in marble, rows of lilies and tulips whose wide-spread petals droop with careless grace, are in low relief. The rooms are shaped like gems; octagons whose surfaces, polished by the workman, repolished by time, play with the light, imprison it, softened and tempered. The ceilings rise in cones, cut in facets, ending in an acute point of crystal. Through them all floats a cool half-light in which gleam the arabesques and flowers, intertwined and involved in a design past all disentanglement; while here and there, the entire thickness of the stone has been tenderly cut out in open-work, making a delicate lace upon the white light of the sky.

Around these rooms are terraces, not edged with balustrades, but surrounded with air only, ending off suddenly at the vertical drop of the high red walls, perpendicular to the river's edge. How often idle queens and odalisques, for ever immured in this gleaming white paradise, have stretched themselves out along this marble surface, to watch the sunlight die, and the slow waters of the Jumna grow pallid, their languid eyes filled with the self-same vision which is mine at this moment! A rosy radiance floats in the immense plain, enwraps all the vague forms. Before me, on a marble cornice, a parrot sits motionless; all is silent in the slow waning of the day. Below, the cold current keeps a little light in motion, among the shallows. There are camps on the shore from which the smoke rises straight. Along a dusty highroad, oxen are drawing heavy wains, whose massive wheels turn slowly. Farther off, a line of camels are moving along with a proud, timid undulation of their swan-like necks, a melancholy procession, half hidden in clouds of dust, half lost in the vaporous light which floods the whole picture.

December 11.

The Taj, as everybody knows, is a mausoleum erected by the Mogul Shah Jahan to the Begum Mumtaz-i-Mahal. It is an irregular octagon (a square with the corners cut off), surmounted by a Persian dome, and having four minarets at its angles. The building itself, which stands upon a marble platform eighteen feet high, having at its angles four tall, cylindrical minarets, is made of blocks of white marble, and rises to a height of two hundred and ten feet. We alight from the carriage in front of a noble portico of red sandstone, pierced by a lofty Moorish archway, covered with white arabesques. We pass under the arch, and the Taj appears in sight, some seventy-five rods away. Probably no masterpiece of architecture produces an equal effect.

At the farther extremity of a marvellous garden, reflected in all its whiteness in a canal of dark water which lies motionless, with clumps of black cypresses and great mounds of crimson flowers on its banks, the perfect structure rises like a vision. It is a floating dream, an aërial thing without weight, so accurate is the balance of the lines and so faint the shadows on the virginal, translucent stone. These black cypresses framing it; these masses of verdure, through which here and there the blue sky is seen; this turf in the strong sunlight, with the sharp, black shadows of the trees falling across it — all these solid things render more unreal the white vision which seems ready to vanish into the light of the sky. I walked toward it along the marble bank of the dark canal, and the mausoleum assumes relief. Approaching nearer, the eye takes more and more delight in the surfaces of the octagonal monument. These are rectangular expanses of polished marble, on which the light rests with a soft, milky lustre. One had no idea that a thing so simple as mere surface could be so beautiful, when it is broad and pure. Then the eye follows the graceful and well-ordered intertwining of great flowers, flowers of onyx and turquoise, incrusted along a projecting part of the building, and the harmony of the delicate chasing, the marble lacework, the springing arches, the notched balustrades, the infinite play of the simple and the decorated.

The garden is the complement of the building, both uniting to form the one artistic conception. The avenues leading to the Taj are bordered with funereal trees, yews and cypresses, that render still whiter the far-off whiteness of the monument. Behind their slender cones, trees of luxuriant foliage are massed, adding depth and opulence to the more sombre growth. The stiff, dark trees, relieved against this light foliage, stirred by the wind, rise, solemn, out of the thickets of roses and the great masses of unknown, perfumed flowers of this solitary garden. Combinations like these are the work of an artist. Broad, open lawns, the crimson cups of flowers, petals of gold, swarms of humming-bees and parti-coloured butterflies bring light and joy into the gloom which befits a cemetery. The place is at once luminous and serious; it has all the rapture of a Musalman paradise, amorous and religious; and the poem in verdure unites with the poem in marble to tell of peace and splendour.

Inside, at first all is darkness, a profound night, with the faint gleaming of a grating of ancient marble, a mysterious lacework around the tombs, extending on and on, with a sepulchral glimmer, a yellowish lustre, as if the light itself were ancient and had been absorbed centuries ago. And the interlacing lines and curves of pallid marble continue, until they vanish into the darkness.

In the centre are the tombs of the lovers, two

small sarcophagi, on which rests a faint light from some unknown source. This is all. There they lie in the silence, surrounded by these perfect things which celebrate their love lasting into death, isolated from all the world by the mysterious marble lace which enwraps them and seems to float around them like a dream.

High above, as if through dense smoke, one sees the dome rise in the darkness, rise and never end; and its walls seem vaporous, the marble blocks unsubstantial. All is aërial here, nothing is real and solid; this is a world of visions. Sounds even are no longer of the earth. A musical note uttered here is repeated, above one's head, in regions which we cannot see. Pure as the voice of an Ariel, it grows fainter, then dies; and suddenly is heard again, far off, glorified, spiritualised, multiplied indefinitely, repeated by countless, remote voices, by an unseen choir of angels who carry it up, ascending higher and higher, until it loses itself in a faint sound which remains continuous, hovering on like the music of a soul over the tomb of the beloved.

I visit the Taj again at noonday. Under a vertical sun the melancholy phantom is dead, the gentle sadness of the mausoleum has disappeared. The great marble table upon which it stands has a blinding glitter. Reflected back and forth from all sides the sunlight multiplies its effect a hundredfold, and some of the façades are like white-hot metal. The incrustations are sparks of living fire, and their hundred red flowers glow like burning coals. The sacred texts and hieroglyphics set in the black marble blaze, as if written by the finger of an angry god. All the mystic rows of lotus and lily, in relief, which before had the softness of yellowed ivory, are now like flames upon the surface. I retreat to the edge of the inclosure, and, dazzled, I see for an instant, relieved against the sky, the incandescent lines and surfaces of the edifice, implacable in its virgin whiteness. Certainly this strict simplicity and the intensity of this light have something Semitic in their effect, like "the flaming sword" of the Bible. The minarets rise into the blue like columns of fire.

All around it is the cool darkness of the overarching trees, where I linger until twilight. This garden is the work of a worshipper, who desired to glorify Allah. It is a place for religious joy: "Let no man who is not pure in heart enter the garden of God," says the Arab text graven above the gate. There are parterres which are heaps of velvet, some of the strange flowers are like bunches of crimson moss. Trunks of trees rise all blue with convolvulus; elsewhere great red stars gleam amid the dark foliage. Among the flowers countless butterflies make a perpetual cloud. Many beautiful little living things, tiny striped squirrels, and birds in abundance, green parrots, brilliant paroquets, a whole little world, splendid, happy, and secure; protected against vultures and hawks by white-clad guards, who with their long peashooters keep away all mischief and cruelty from this place of peace.

Upon the surface of the motionless water, waterlilies and the lotus outline their stiff petals, seeming to rest solidly upon the dark mirror. Between the dense masses of foliage there are glimpses of English lawns all flooded with sunlight, and of spaces of blue sky sometimes traversed by a triangle of white storks; and now and then the far-off vision of the phantom tomb, a sad, virginal ghost. How calm and splendid is this solitude, full of a pleasure at once intoxicating and serious! It is the beauty, the love, the sunlight of Asia, of which Shelley dreamed!

December 12.

After three days devoted to marble palaces, one wearies of exquisite things. And so, this morning, instead of taking the railway train, I take a carriage, that I may go to see a big bit of country, the real Hindu land, not merely from a railway train, but loitering along the roads at pleasure, through the villages, far from the marvels that tourists visit. We drive slowly, and are the whole day in making the thirty miles between Agra and Muttra.

There is nothing very noticeable in the appearance of the country; the palms have disappeared; there are little bushy trees, suggestive of the apple orchards of Normandy; and the plain is spotted with patches of russet grass and tall yellow reeds. This December morning is like the very early hours of one of our beautiful June days, still and bright. A herd of meagre buffaloes goes past us,

M

their long black heads bent resignedly toward the ground, and for hours these are the only living creatures that we see.

Later we come to a group of little huts, one of those Hindu villages whose aspect has not changed in three thousand years, where there has been always the same calm, primitive life since the beginning of history. These villages would be an interesting study, for they have kept the ancient traditions of our Aryan races. Their organisation is like that of the primitive Greek and Germanic communes. There is no written law: all is regulated by immemorial and unexplained custom; the whole political life is instinctive, as in an anthill. It is a natural grouping, the true form of grouping of Hindu society. The Mongols, and, before their time, the Pathans, were able to destroy the native monarchies and establish everywhere their own rule. But the village was a molecule too minute to attract attention, too small and coherent to be broken up; and it is this which has enabled the Hindu world, the Hindu spirit, Hinduism itself, to subsist, through centuries of tyrannies and exterminations.

I can see in passing only the outdoor aspect: these are scenes of other days which carry one's thought back to the Homeric age. A group of women around a well, "each bearing the amphora, one hand on the hip," naked babies wallowing in the dust, little girls clad with a single piece of red stuff, which leaves half the childish figure bare; with the timid, frightened mien of kittens they run back as we come near. The potter, seated on the ground, is kneading his clay; old wrinkled women, with skins like parchment, are pounding rice in a mill of rough stone; a little naked group of scholars are gathered around the master, who is humming in a kind of plain-song, as he unrolls a manuscript. At the threshold of a door, a man sitting on his heels, with the air of a patient martyr, has given himself into the hands of a barber, who is tenderly shaving his head. There are beggars, who might be centenarians, wretched, fleshless creatures, tottering on their sticks, squealing as they hold out a black paw. In the midst of the road, shoemakers, sitting in a ring, ply the awl, and smoke at a hookah whose mouthpiece is passed from hand to hand. At the end of the village, very neatly arranged on little tables, are a few dainty bits of sugar-cane, and fresh leaves of green betel twisted into horns.

Soon it is left behind us, this little world, somewhat stirred by our passage, and we are again upon the highroad which cuts the plain with its straight line. Occasionally we pass a string of camels; they move along with a soft, haughty step, turning from side to side their meagre, thick-lipped heads at the end of the long, flexible necks, which curve and undulate, with the rider pitching about on the top of the backbone. Then, bands of peasants, the head and the waist wrapped with white; and women, whose arms and ankles are cuirassed with porcelain bracelets; and little donkeys, invisible under their huge loads. Sometimes there are enormous rude wains with heavy wheels; the pole, a little tree roughly squared, like those which the barbarian peoples must have used in their migrations. These are drawn by great white oxen, big hunchbacked oxen, with short muscular necks, their horns painted gold colour or blue. Tranquil amid the buzzing of the eager flies, their eyes half closed, they move along with a stupid air of triumph, as if they knew very well that they were gods.

On every side are the great, shining fields full of green harvests; and the brilliant garments of the women who are reaping seem like scattered poppies and violets just visible in the dense growth.

December 13.

Last evening by moonlight we reached the dâk bungalow of Muttra. It is an abrupt return into the world of Hinduism. Here Vishnu was incarnated under the form of Krishna, and the city is consecrated to the worship of this hero. By turns, Hindu, Greek, Buddhist, Musalman, and then Hindu again, Muttra has always been one of the religious capitals of Asia; it is celebrated in the Baghavata Purana. In 404 a Chinese pilgrim counted here twenty monasteries and three thousand Buddhist monks. Five hundred years later the Musalmans invaded the country, and the Brahmanic pagodas which had been reared upon the ruins of the Buddhist monasteries were destroyed by the conquerors. From 1017 to the date of the English conquest, incessantly trodden down by the Muhammadan chiefs, Hinduism, like a sturdy and deep-rooted plant, never ceased to spring up again; and no destruction could put an end to its incessant efflorescence in temples and chapels.

In the eighteenth century Aurungzebe levelled them all to the ground, and built mosques out of the material. Fortunately the French traveller Tavernier had seen the chief pagoda, and his description reminds one of the temples of the south, those of Madura and Trichinopoli. "From base to summit the exterior is covered with figures of rams, monkeys, and elephants in stone, with niches in which are monsters, and with windows up to the height of the domes and balconies. Statues of monsters are in a ring around these domes; this collection of hideous images is frightful to see." Having paid two rupees, he was permitted to behold the god himself. "The Brahmans opened a door, and I saw a kind of altar covered with old brocade, on which stood the great idol. The head was of black marble, and the eyes appeared to be rubies. The body and arms were entirely hidden by a robe of red velvet. Two smaller idols, white-faced, were placed at the two sides."

He is to be seen everywhere here, Krishna,* the dark god, the blue god. All the religious pictures adorning the stalls represent him, surrounded by his women, playing on the pipe, a smile in his enamelled eyes. He is the popular

* Probably a god of the black, pre-Aryan races, absorbed by Hinduism.

divinity of India, the good-humoured, laughing god, friendly to men. He was born of a woman, and countless poems relate his marvellous childhood, the wickedness of the king who sought him out among the other children to destroy him, the humility of his life as a little shepherd, his flute songs during the rains and in the hot season, the instruction that he gave the Brahmans while yet a child, his sports in the sacred waters of the Jumna, his dances with the *gopis*—the young and charming cow-herd girls of Muttra—his amours in the tropical forest. Meanwhile, miracles proclaim his divinity. He destroys dragons and demons. One day, as he is dancing with his young companions, he becomes multiple, and each girl has him in her arms. He raises a mountain for a shelter to the human race against aërial genii. He charms all things, movable and immovable, the entire creation. "At the sound of his flute, the young girls hastened hither, happy and also sad with love. The cows, hearing this flute, stood motionless, the grass in their mouths; the little calves with delighted faces forgot to feed. The gazelles stretched their necks; the soft melody disturbed ascetics and wise men. Rivers turned back like snakes, and ceased flowing. Arrested in their flight, birds perched at his side, jealous of his music, and, *with closed eyes*, listened to the sounds of his flute." Later, he preaches gentleness and self-abnegation; forbids pride and selfishness; fights against "the Me sentiment"; defends the weak, and teaches the brotherhood of all mankind.

This is a singular divinity, with traits of Orpheus, Adonis, Hercules, and of Jesus, at once ascetic and sensual. To die to the world, to forget one's self for love of the divinity or of one's neighbour, this is his doctrine; a teaching which would seem more fitting for the austere and gentle Buddha than for Krishna; but on the other hand, with an inexplicable contradiction, he teaches a free abandonment to all the gratifications of opulent nature. A poor humpbacked creature, having poured lotus perfume upon Krishna's feet, rises, erect and beautiful as a queen, and all the pollution of her heart is washed away.

Then men proclaim him divine; and, in the universal homage which hails him, Krishna, the shepherd, disappears; his human form is dissolved, the "illusion" which concealed him vanishes; through the veil which covered him appears a vague, radiant, pantheistic idea, a universal power which the whole choir of nature adores: "Thou art he who createst; thou art the creating force, O sacred Master; it is thou, O Lord, who makest the succession of births and deaths; thy incarnations have revealed thee to man; thou art the productive force, thou art Brahma. The fourteen worlds are in thy mouth, as fruit is between the teeth of a monkey. If thou withdrawest them, who can compel thee to emit them anew? If thou hidest thyself, all becomes confusion, and the destroyed bodies have no longer a covering to enwrap them. As water dwells in the lotus-leaf, as the perfume in the flower, as fire in the wood, as water in milk, thus thou, in thine own form, art in the depths of all being."

These pantheistic flashes strike abruptly through the descriptive luxuriance of the poem ; and then the veil, for a moment lifted, falls ; the metaphysical world, of which there was a glimpse, is again shut away ; and around us closes in " the illusion " of nature, all full of light and life. " The green buds of the santal tremble at the extremity of the branches like limpid drops of ambrosia. When they heard the sound of his flute, the lotus, the jasmine, the pandanas, and the champak quivered in their hearts. The flowers became the colour of the ointment of antimony and of red lead; they shivered, they were afraid, the blue and white flowers." The simplest of these idyls, the most ardent and splendid, represents the young divinity with the shepherd girls of Muttra. They cannot behold without rapture his beautiful dark brow, they languish for love of him ; " and like white lotus flowers whose root is wounded under the water, the moonlight of their downcast faces shines with pallid splendour." It is a poem like one of the luminous, voluptuous nights of India. It is like a southern jungle, where, in an air dense with stupefying perfumes, butterflies, strangely splendid, fly heavily, and impenetrable tropical climbers bar your path, all rustling and throbbing with unseen life. Here and there, the strong upward thrust of a cocoanut - palm leads your glance upward, and through a gap in the dense foliage you can see for an instant the dazzling, creative orb which fills all the sombre forest with its heat, and from the inert slime calls forth this world of living things.

December 14.

Upon the Jumna.—I arrive too late to witness the sacred dip of all the population. The men have gone, and only a few groups of women remain. Young girls, the slender torso rising out of a blue drapery which falls from the hips, their arms lifted, the wrists crossed upon the head, standing erect on the steps that lead down into the water, watch our boat as it passes. Others, stooping, are entirely concealed by the harmonious folds of some ample material; only the dark face is visible beneath the light drapery resting on the curve of the head. One little girl, throwing off her garment, stands quite nude; she stoops toward the water, half bent over it. Another child, still younger, clasps close with her slender arms the pink muslin drapery enveloping her from the head to the silver-banded ankles. It is graceful and charming. Some have risen and slowly lift to their heads the heavy copper vases filled with river water, and the movement of the arms and the torso is noble and graceful. The faces are of a pure oval, a little rounded, of a beautiful bronze tint, caressed by the blackness of their waving hair; with something serious and sombre, almost classic, in their features, yet not without warmth and tenderness. They are here in great numbers, small and large, chattering and laughing, playing

with the water much like their predecessors, the
Hindu girls beloved of Krishna; washing their
hands and arms, and their hair; taking off and
putting on their great veils; spending the whole
day in the coolness of the broad, deep river. In
this light, with these simple draperies, the motion
or gesture of these young girls gives one pleasure,
a bare arm lifted, the head slowly turning upon
the young neck, a bent figure becoming erect. It
is indeed a very simple and quiet pleasure to watch
this play of noble colours and of human outlines
on the bank of the translucent water, upon the
luminous marble.

An hour's drive brings us to Bindrabun, which
is also a sacred city. Holy places are numerous
in this classic corner of India. The shores of the
Jumna at all these points are celebrated in the
great epics.

At Bindrabun, as at Muttra, the monkeys swarm;
they frolic in the streets and accompany the inhabitants to their matutinal dip. Now they gather,
mingling with the inquisitive human crowd, to see
us arrive; and the rapid winking of their eyes is
much more intelligent than the slow, stupid gaze
of these Hindus.

Men and monkeys live here the same idle and
abstemious life. They eat the same cereals, they
dwell in the same houses; the former usually
established inside, the latter more commonly clinging to the balconies, or perched upon the roof,
where they are quite at their ease, the lucky rascals!
teasing each other, or cleaning each other in the

sunshine; the theories of Darwin are put in practice in Bindrabun, and the human being is peacefully domesticated with his "poor relations."

Two great temples are in process of building, at the expense of the rajah. One is nearly done, and will be completed in two years; the cost is estimated at twenty-five lacs of rupees. The architect, the workmen, the sculptors, are all natives. He is the greatest independent prince in India, this rajah of Jaipur, who supplies the money; and the god, with his hundred million worshippers, is the most popular of divinities. Without any doubt, Hinduism is very much alive, as any man may see who regards these thousands of labourers hewing stone for the greater honour of Krishna.

The architect, delighted to receive a European visitor, shows me his plans, which appear very scientific and geometrical. He explains to me, later, the detail of the inferior divinities whose niches will surround the statue of Krishna. I observe that he says, God, not *the* god, in speaking of the latter. "This," he says, "is God's dining-room. Every day the value of a hundred or two hundred rupees in food is served to him here, by the rajah's order; and it is then distributed among the poor."

But this is an interesting rajah! He is a civilised person, I am told, and to him Jaipur owes its University. Why, then, does he build this temple to Krishna? What idea, vague or distinct, does he have of this divinity and his incarnations; of the entire multitude of the Hindu gods; of their avatars and of their sacred animals? Is his faith in any degree sincere? Does he go beyond the mere conformity to custom and to the religion of his country? Is he conscious of any lack of harmony between his ideas and his religious needs?

I am glad to see how the buildings of Agra were constructed. These workmen are making a marble lacework, in imitation of those airy balustrades, that exquisite guipure which gives the lightness of a dream to the Mongol edifices. Fifteen men, bending over a block of stone, are cutting it out with jewellers' tools, copying a complicated design of interlaced leaves and stems. This being completed, they turn the stone, and work from the other side, to meet the first work; with what care, with what infinite precision, may be understood when you reflect that on the two sides the flowers and stems must perfectly correspond. Work like this is done only at great loss; one block of marble in three is spoiled. I also saw the incrustation with gems; they use the lamp, as jewellers do in setting precious stones.

There are four thousand workmen. The average wage is four annas a day. The temple will have been five years in building. Notwithstanding the expense, and the length of the labour, it is already evident that this structure will not equal the perfect edifices of the Mongol emperors. The marble here is used only as a facing; the Mongol work, on the contrary, was absolutely sincere, made of the same rare material, polished with the same care, in the invisible portions of the building as in its exterior.

It was not done for the purpose of being admired; it was an end in itself, like a prayer or like a grand psalm. Provinces of men were laid waste to provide means; at it, nations wore out their hands and their knees. The labour lasted a half-century; and the building was reared at what a cost of human suffering! But the work was absolutely beautiful. In like manner there is required the long and silent labour of a thousand invisible roots, of all the obscure vessels and concealed tissues, a slow elaboration from the juices of the whole plant, to expand a flower and give to it its subtle perfume.

CHAPTER VII

DELHI JAIPUR

December 15.

YOU perceive at once the great capital. The English city lies among the trees : broad avenues, elegant villas, vast gardens. In the distance, crowded blocks of houses, minarets, Hindu cones, rise on every side, bristling against the sky ; this is the native city.

One begins with the public edifices. Probably my eye is blasé ; I see nothing approaching the perfection of Agra. The fort has been spoiled by the English occupation ; in many places the precious stones have been dug out, and their place supplied with red or green wax. In general, the plan is the same as that of the fort at Agra. Very high exterior walls, extensive courts for parades and shows with elephants, sumptuous halls decorated with gold scrollwork, their walls incrusted with jewelled birds and flowers, harems which are exquisite as a dream : all this I have already seen in Akbar's capital. "If Paradise can be found in the world, it is here !" says a Persian inscription.

No doubt this fortress, also, shelters a paradise of idle delights ; there is the same abundance of mosaic work, of marble trellises, of sinuous lotus stems and flowers in relief; there are the mysterious, shadowy bathrooms, and the terraces without balustrades, whence you will see the sun go down across a reedy plain, all resembling Agra. The little mosque for the women is a jewel in marble that would seem to have been cut from a single block; the three domes are like pearls. The whole thing should be kept in a jewel-case.

Better still, however, do I like the great mosque, the most beautiful in India, it is said, and, probably, in all Asia. Broad stairs that, with a single oblique bound, fall in sheets of marble; above, a court paved with polished alabaster, white, dazzling, which looks as if it were made from one immense lustrous stone; on three sides of this court a deep gallery, sustained by three rows of pillars; at the right and left, stiff slender minarets: this is the grand Muhammadan style. An astonishing severity and simplicity of lines: a general effect of something dominant and supreme. The towers in their simplicity rise high above the city, imperious as a conqueror. It was here that the emperor, attended by his nobles and his people, standing upon the pavement, facing a white wall, used to listen to the harsh sentences of the Koran, the fierce and ardent law. Thereafter, he would order the sack of a Hindu city; then, build mosques, with the materials of the destroyed pagodas; and then glorify in his heart the proud name of Allah.

The priests of Allah are not proud. The high-priest, with silent gravity, showed us relics of Muhammad, a sandal, a hair of his beard. As I

bent my head before him, full of respect and
gratitude, suddenly he held out his hand. Cheddy
Lal, who has charge of the baksheesh, presented
him with three annas. Silent as before, the high-
priest bowed, thanking us with a dignified gesture.

However, he keeps up appearances. The Hindu
dealers are more demonstrative. At the railway
station, twenty shawl-merchants worry the unlucky
traveller. They accompany him to his hotel, running beside the carriage, climbing on the step,
clinging to the door, gesticulating, assailing him
with a hail of cards, inundating him with a never-
ending flow of obsequious speech. At the hotel,
one is not rid of them. They install themselves
upon the verandah, they mount guard outside your
bedroom, outside the dining-room : you come out,
they rush upon you; it becomes a scuffle, you
show your fists, brandish your stick to get through.
The first encounters being over, you suppose
yourself at peace; take notice that all the time
piercing eyes are on the watch for you. At six
in the morning, you awaken. Instantly, at the
other end of the great white bedroom, a door is
set ajar a few inches; five arms are pushed
through, brandishing stuffs, slippers, caps. They
saw you fall asleep; they saw you wake. Some
conceal themselves, following you in the street
on the opposite side-walk, waiting till you are
tired, alone, unprotected, and seize the oppor-
tune moment to present themselves.

A few minutes ago, sauntering in the great bazaar,
I accompanied Cheddy to a shawl-dealer's, who this

morning very nearly got himself crushed by my *garry* in his endeavour to obtain the promise of a visit. We find a fat man, of gentle face, seated upon cushions, drinking coffee with some friends. Upon our entrance he springs to his feet, he runs back and forth, he whirls about me, he envelops me in his gesticulations. In the twinkling of an eye, before I know how he has done it, we have each had a cup of coffee, and are seated before a bale, which he unrolls with the agility of a monkey; out of it emerge, as if by magic, rare silks, embroideries in gold, which he holds up in the light, with which he drapes himself, with which he drapes me, with all sorts of feminine airs and graces. "I want you, sir, to see this beautiful thing. What do you think of it? Is it not beautiful? Put it aside. You look at me. Don't you think it will do for the young lady at home?" The abrupt English, the colourless accent, are something amazing; but the short sentences accumulate with deafening ardour. In three minutes it appears that I have made my selection: a shawl, a little rug; only a hundred and fifty rupees. I know Hindu dealers, and I have sense enough left to offer half. Almost before I have mentioned the sum, my man cries: "Let's toss up!" That is to say, the price shall be a hundred and fifty rupees if the coin falls head up; seventy-five, if tails. I refuse. At once the things are mine, and the transaction is so promptly made that it is clear the Hindu is not the loser.

Now, satisfied, he becomes calm; and, in another tone of voice, enters upon a new subject. It appears that this evening, at the hotel, I am to have the honour of meeting a duchess. All the shawl-dealers have been on the alert since her arrival; and each one, watching her, keeps watch upon his rivals as well. My man begs that I will speak of him at the *table d'hôte.* "Give and take," he says; and to persuade me, offers as a present a cap whose silver he exhibits in the light. Treating me as a friend, he confides the fact that he has a stock of shawls worth three lacs of rupees, showing me also diplomas from English Expositions.

It is easy to see that these Orientals do not know the feeling of shame. It appears that honour and conscience are products of the West, which cannot be elaborated here. All beg for baksheesh with clasped hands; and in the most serious and the richest of them, you may find a beggar and a thief.

December 16.

Taking a carriage, I go to visit the Kutab-Minar, the great tower which is ten miles distant from Delhi.

Our road is an Asiatic Appian Way. Ruins from every century, left by three races and three religions, strew a great, melancholy plain. Fragments of ancient Hindu Delhi, of Afghan Delhi, of Mongol Delhi, cover a dead extent of seventy miles square. Slowly, in the course of centuries, the city has changed its site, as a river changes its bed. As far as the eye can see, among the withered brushwood, rise ruinous domes and broken columns. These yellowish heaps are the remains of Indra-Partha, the city of Indra, for which the five brothers of Mahabarata fought, three thousand years ago ! Farther on, a granite pier, covered with faded characters, proclaims the edicts of the Buddhist king Asoka. Everywhere, like tombs in a cemetery, are heaped the fragments of Mongol art, monumental mausolea, domes surrounded with kiosks, all discoloured by time, brought to a uniform tint with the sad and withered vegetation, all taken back by nature. A few tombs are as imposing as Akbar's at Secundra, and rise solitary amid the arid steppe. The blue peacocks wandering about them are the only living things that haunt the spot. Generations have swarmed here, and of their dead life there remains this imperceptible residue ; as it takes centuries of forest growth to make a thin stratum of coal. The Vedic age, the Brahmanic age, the Buddhist age, the first Musalman dynasties, the Mongol epoch—each historic period has left, so to speak, its small deposit.

This is the history of the Kutab : four ancient Hindu forts, still quite recognisable, once inclosed a great city with its Buddhist temples, where monks in yellow robes with shaven heads went peacefully to and fro ; of this period there remains a huge iron post, having on it Sanskrit inscriptions. About the year 1000, over the Himalayan wall came the first Musalman hordes. The city was razed, and from the stone of its great temple was built a mosque, whose ruins lie around us.* Here is a

* About 1193.

triple colonnade in which have been recognised the old Buddhist piers and the patient, complicated, confused labour of the poor Hindu workman. These stones are very deeply cut, and are loaded with chasing, half effaced by time. Here and there symbolic figures have been mutilated by the higher morality of the conquering race. By degrees you accustom yourself to read what the blurred stone has to say, the lines grow clearer. You can discern processions of gods surrounded by guards and worshippers; then animals, tigers, monkeys, and elephants, which very early seem to have greatly attracted the Hindu mind. These thousands of blocks of stone, once forming irregular chapels and grooved roofs, the Musalmans, later, employed in colonnades, rectangular galleries, simple geometric rows. Upon the great bare walls, cabalistic figures, letters like birds' tracks, thundered against the blasphemer. Above it all, dominating the immense cemetery of the plain, inviolate by time, the Kutab sends up, two hundred and fifty feet high, its shaft of red stone and white marble. From its top, six centuries ago, when yonder sun sank behind that horizon, the sharp cry of the muezzin was wont to break the silence of the great plains.

JAIPUR, *December* 17.

At eight in the morning I take the Rajputana express; a curious phrase that, and significant of many things! The exteriors of this civilisation of English India are very brilliant. Except at Benares, where you see exactly the same spectacles that were to be seen two thousand years ago, in all the cities that I have visited so far, in Calcutta, Lucknow, Cawnpur, Agra, the beauty and neatness of the avenues, the wealth of the villas, the luxury of private and public gardens, the comfort and number of hotels, the multitude of carriages, the grand scale of the railway stations, would do honour to a great European city. The question remains to what depth this English life has penetrated the Hindu world.

All around is the same vast plain, where slender grasses grow feebly in the sand. This is the limit of the vegetable world. A few leagues westward the desert, the gloomy, yellow waste, begins.

And now, the sharp and simple outlines of sandy mountains rise here and there from the level of the plain like precipitous islets emerging from the sea. There are no spurs, no preliminary undulations of the ground. I observed in the Red Sea a similar effect; the promontory of Sinai, emerging on the edge of the blue horizon designed in the arid air an outline no less clear and hard. From time to time, long lines of camels announced that the nomad world, the world of the tent, was near.

About two o'clock, at Ulwar, the aspect of the country becomes more fresh and animated. Great grey monkeys are playing in the grass. Near the station are the eternal blue peacocks, which seem to people all the North-west of India. While the train stops, I observe a group of women leaning against a gate. The youngest, wrapped in a red garment, has the beautiful oval face and the colourless complexion of a Florentine of the Renaissance. The features are of classic regularity, with that inexpressible gravity and dignity we meet so often here among low-caste women. There is nothing savage or inferior in these types, of the purest Aryan stamp. This one stood motionless, so calm, so serious, her great sombre eyes full of concentrated passion.

Two British soldiers, of the Scots Greys, came into my compartment. The fine types of race! Each man as tall and stout as two Hindus; solid, well set-up, buttoned tight in his grey jacket. Nor are they simply fine, healthy animals. This flesh is all muscle, hardened by training. Their faces, under the Scotch caps, are full of frankness and honesty. Features strong, well cut, expressive, complexions clear, gestures to the point, and made quietly. Their moral and physical training has given them a certain repose of manner, a certain dignity, a stamp of "the gentleman." During the eight hours' journey from Ulmar to Jaipur they remained silent and impassive, speaking once only, to refuse a glass of wine! Evidently they are "teetotalers."

I was looking over a book by a Bengali on the English establishment in India, and from time to time my eyes left the book to observe the two Scots; they aided me in understanding it. In that peculiar mental condition, stimulated and yet slightly confused, which is caused by sleeplessness and continuous, rapid motion on the railway; in that half-fever which accelerates at the same time that it blurs the associations of ideas, their faces interested me strangely. I seemed to see, in these soldiers that chance had thus thrown in my way, not individual personalities, but the type itself of the race now mistress in the peninsula—the pure, complete, developed type; and their faces were to me as a living expression of the British soul. I could read in them the calm, decided will, the tenacity, the habit of self-control, the enthusiastic pride underlying the other qualities, and those practical aptitudes which, in England, have doubled the active force of the human being and his grasp upon realities.

And with this, whiffs of England came into my head; separate, simple images coming, one by one: a November evening, in a little chapel on the Devonshire coast; outside, the black water, splashing in the darkness; here, the whole village crowded into a hall of bare pine boards, all heads turned toward one of their own people who is preaching; hard faces, ploughed with wrinkles; rows of old fishermen clasping their Bibles with gaunt, trembling hands: then, the yellow atmosphere of the city, at the hour when the streets are black with the crowd: again, young men in white flannel throwing balls in greyish fields: long lines of great misty vessels on a dull-coloured river, whose leaden mirror gleams dolefully through a fog: brick cities, drowned in a sluggish smoke rising from ten thousand factory chimneys.

Then these confused images blend and disappear; and, without transition, as if one turned the mental stereoscope, in a rosy light, a great muddy river appears; the divine Ganges is flowing past its two thousand pagodas, at Benares, and on its banks the inert crowd of Brahmans, sitting on their heels.

The Thames below London, the Ganges at Benares — in the presence of this contrast one measures the abyss separating the two races which here we see placed together. In the depths of the English soul, as great Englishmen have made it visible to us—Cromwell or Milton, Wordsworth or Carlyle—and as we see it still more clearly in their works of art, where the type, pure and clear, is thrown into stronger relief than in the real world, in Robinson Crusoe or in Tom Tulliver, one perceives a strong and almost changeless *personality;* a steadfast will, supported by a few permanent and powerful sentiments, a solid axis, on which everything rests. They all conceive life as a series of prescribed acts, whose aim is to ameliorate the condition, to augment the well-being, and to perfect the moral nature. This ideal, with an admirable enthusiasm, and with a narrowness of mind which seems the penalty of her active virtues, England sets before India; multiplying schools for boys and girls, colleges, and universities; and ruining herself with missionaries. It is said that the results are meagre, and that English culture produces only miserable failures: Chunder Dutt, the Bengali whom I have just now been reading, is a specimen of the converted babu; he imagines no other model than the English. Hence, he demands the complete application of the English moral code; he denounces feminine dress and the promiscuous dip in the sacred rivers. Here is the idea of this Bengali, who aspires to be the English clergyman : to have the sacred shore of the ancient river divided by barriers and placards, " Ladies on one side, gentlemen on the other." But this invention denotes a lack of culture and the critical faculty. Chunder Dutt, who has read Macaulay, has not read Renan. However, this scandal is not about to cease. The success of the missionaries in India is really very small. It has been estimated that every Hindu conversion costs England a thousand pounds sterling; and however sincere the convert may be, and however hard he may strive to make himself as an Englishman, it is certain that all he can do is only to assume a disguise. For the intellectual and moral habits of a people, like the organs of a plant, are conditioned upon a certain combination of circumstances which is infinitely complex, and in which the principal element is the entire series of its antecedents. All their past has made them what they are.

Ah ! ancient ascetics, profound dreamers, who sought, twenty centuries ago, to tear away the rainbow-hued veil which illusion weaves over the dark reality; who renounced all personal desire, to shelter yourselves in indifference and immobility; with what a smile of disdainful pity would you regard that Western race which now rules in your land ! *They* do not believe that the world is a dream, these new-comers. They have not ceased from saying: "I am." They rejoice in their strength, and their will obtains its gratification. They act, they build upon this world which they believe of rock, and you believe is shifting sand. What would you say of their haste and fever? What would you say of these ships loaded with this world's goods; of these trains which devour the distance, as if it were of any consequence to change one's place, to go any whither? But, above all, what would you say of this meagre English philosophy, which vegetates in yonder land of fogs where there is no luxuriance of nature; and of this theistic heresy, which they propose to naturalise in the home of broad speculation? This, at least, is certain: you would make no attempt to enlighten them, blinded by Maya. You would leave them to their ignorant goings to and fro, to their pride; and, slowly closing your eyes, you would return with delight to your solitary dream, to your tranquillising contemplation of the eternal and motionless!

It is certain that the English stratum is greatly in evidence in India, even in the states which are independent. There is always an "English Church," severe and unadorned, like those which keep guard over the country in England. At the spacious railway stations, colonists in shooting jackets are reading eight-paged "papers." Placards announce "a match between the cricketers of Lucknow and the champions of Allahabad"; or races at Ahmedabad and Baroda. Other placards advertise a machine which turns out ten thousand bottles of soda-water daily. Ouida's romances and those of Walter Besant lie on a counter.

Meantime women, clad as were the Hindu contemporaries of Homer, their ankles, ears, and noses adorned with rings, carry stoneware jars. Warriors go by, bristling with sabres, loaded with bucklers; and we are upon the territory of a prince who, at Bindrabun, is erecting a pagoda to Krishna.

December 18.

At Calcutta, English India; at Benares, the India of the Brahmans; at Agra, the India of the Grand Moguls; here, the India of the rajahs, the India of novels and the opera—fairy-like and incredible. The Rajputana is a very ancient Hindu kingdom, resembling those which covered the peninsula before the Musalman establishments in the early centuries of our era. It has never been conquered. Against the diverse races who have ruled in India, the Rajputs have maintained their independence. They are still the Aryan people that they were in the fabulous time of the Ramáyana. Across a hundred and thirty-nine generations, the rajah claims descent from the sun, who was father of the great Rama; and he still governs according to the law of Manu, as did the Hindu kings, his ancestors, who lived before Cæsar. The nobles are of a race equally good, like himself descendants of the sun and moon, and the early history of the great Rajput families is lost in the night of time.

The population, organised, as in the primitive days, in clans, in tribes, is of noble race, of white race. Every Rajput is by birth a *Kshatriya*, belonging to that caste of Aryan warriors who recognise no superiors but the Brahmans. Hence a man of the country esteems himself the equal of his princes. He is called "the king's son." His character is proud, manly, honourable; he has a horse, a lance, and a shield; in battle he follows the chief of his clan, and loyally stands by his father, the king, in defence of the gods and the country.

Even from the hotel, outside the city, you recognise a very original world. Low, yellowish hills, all crowned with strongholds and crenellated towers, encircle the horizon. A mediæval stage-scene was not a thing to be expected in the tropics. Along the road, through the crowd of little donkeys, past troops of women who sing as they walk, horsemen, mounted on fine Arab steeds, a round buckler at the belt, a sabre at the side, coiffed with red turbans, their great beards parted in the middle and spreading out, flattened and bristling, at the right and left, prance with an air of the most audacious courage. Nothing of that gentle, indolent, dreamy expression which I have so often seen in India. This is a very active world: people on foot, horsemen, camels, elephants, heavy carts, small donkeys, crowd the roads, and all this crowd is noisy, and glittering in the dust and sunshine.

After half an hour on the way, we arrive at the postern of the fortified wall surrounding the city.

I pass under high bastions, cross a drawbridge, then a little inner courtyard, where kneeling camels are waiting to be unloaded, and of a sudden I emerge into the scenery of an opera, misty, light, fantastic, charming, indescribable.

The first thing you are conscious of is the pink colour of the picture. Let the reader supply this colour as I attempt to describe what I beheld. Let him imagine a street a hundred and twenty feet wide, and two miles long, bordered with pink houses, pink temples, pink palaces, pink bell-towers, and pavilions, the pink a most delicate rose-colour, and this street so straight that to its very end you see the houses, shops, façades, in perfect alignment succeeding each other, growing indistinct in the distance, vanishing in a mist of this same extraordinary pink. There is not a spot of dark colour anywhere, not a European carriage, nothing but the multi-coloured twinkling of the crowd. On the side-walks to the right and left, as far as you can see, it is a bazaar in the open air, a row of dealers seated on the ground, and, upon blue and red rugs which are spread out upon the pavement, a great display of shining objects—slippers embroidered with silver, piles of oranges and bananas, painted images, stuffs splashed with sunshine. To right and left all is graceful and luminous; one could spend a day walking through the streets, and it would be a pleasure to retain an exact memory of each detail. The eye cannot be satisfied with seeing. Vainly I cry to my coachman: *Hasta! hasta!* (Slowly! slowly!) we still go too fast; and to his great disgust I leave the carriage, that I may saunter at will.

Rajput nobles and functionaries, adorned as for a play, clothed in embroidery, loaded with feathers and jewels, their imposing beards skilfully spread out fanwise; handsome, well-groomed horses; romantic soldiers, with shield and sword; students, guards, women of the people, sometimes carrying a naked baby astride on the hip: all go by in a light mist which is the evaporation of the heavy dew.

From the edge of their stalls, the little dealers stretch out their arms to me, offering, with a pretty smile, marble statuettes, pictures of gods hastily daubed, yet not without spirit and expression. The walls are all tattooed with designs in blue: elephants, leopards, trees, locomotives, Europeans very stiff, buttoned tight in ridiculous frockcoats. There are grown men flying kites and running about the streets like schoolboys. And all this whimsical people, laughing and playing, this boyish, artistic people, seem created by a poet's comic caprice, in a dream-world where all must be light, droll, gay, airy, and none of the sad and hateful realities of life should remain.

In this world men live like brothers with the animals, those good souls that are more simple and more tranquil than we. See the strings of little donkeys with their little trot, the gentle camels of slow and undulating gait, lifting their long, womanish necks above the crowd; the flocks of grey monkeys upon the roofs; the peaceful cows with great greenish horns, themselves white, statuesque, as if carved in marble. There are small dogs, coloured yellow, blue, or pink. Further, in a large open square, a crowded population of pigeons, lighting by myriads, cover the ground with a dense, undulating, bluish floor, which opens as the heavy bulk of an elephant, caparisoned with red, passes through. Among all these living animals, here and there are altars for their worship; tiny tabernacles filled with little bulls, little elephants, little monkeys. This square is at the intersection of two streets, which meet at right angles, the other street just as broad, as straight, as pink as the one we have followed. Here, at the foot of temples guarded by elephants in stone, there is a great confusion of passers-by, of flowers, of donkeys, camels, horsemen, and dealers. Among the crowd of pigeons picking up their food, there are a hundred cows peacefully reposing, indifferent to all the stir around them; boys, standing, hold up tall branches that fill the space with verdure: these the worshippers buy, and lay them before the cows, who accept this homage as their due, and munch serenely. From the tops of trees hang earthen vases green with moss, on which alight flocks of parrots, their pretty round heads ringed with red.

Suddenly a prancing of horses. What is this proud cavalcade which comes into the square? The fine animals with their lustrous coats, the handsome cavaliers with glittering weapons! This is the brother of the rajah, followed by his barons, preceded by his men-at-arms, who run on foot, carrying halberds. A velvet cap over one ear, in a green embroidered tunic, the prince manages his capering horse. For an instant I see him, a bold and noble face, which shows the grand ancestry, the good blood, the instinct of command. He is a true Kshatriya, lineal descendant of the first conquerors of India.

Meanwhile, the elephants come back to their stable. Here are seven, rugged and sombre colossi, taciturn philosophers, full of slowness, superior to all the beings who are scurrying about them. One by one they disappear under a porch, brushing the ground with their trunks, each with three cornacs on his massive head, with its huge flapping ears. Bending the knee, as with a human gait, gently setting down their big, soft feet, they pass, silent as shadows. What profound thought in those sad, heavy heads, and how they ignore this inferior population of men and beasts who scatter before them! It is comprehensible, as you see them, that Ganesa, the wise god, should have an elephant's head.

At every instant the pictures change; I try to note this one as it flies: before a lofty door of the palace, into which disappear pachyderms, camels, a whole city full of men, the air is thick with falcons. They whirl and scream before the red image of the elephant god, which sleeps in a niche over the porch; and shrill trumpets make a Hindu music.

All around the square are temples, monuments,

university, palaces; one, among the rest, of a singularly vivid rose-colour, rising in the form of a pyramid, bristles with a nine-storied façade, composed of a hundred bell-turrets, and sixty-four projecting windows, adorned with colonnettes and balconies, pierced in open-work with countless flowers cut out in the stone; a vaporous, airy, impossible construction. This is the palace of the Wind—the palace of the Wind? How enchanting the name! There is, also, on a beautiful little hill outside the city, the palace of the Clouds; and on another hill the temple of the Sun. The rose-coloured gate at the other end of Jaipur is called the gate of Rubies. This is clearly the city of a fairy tale. A trumpet-call! A brazen voice which makes one look around. Running very rapidly, comes a merry funeral train; comes the corpse closely wrapped in white gauze; come the bearers who carry it, slung from bamboos; comes the family, leaping, clashing cymbals, screaming out the sacred syllable: "Ram! Ram!" They have all gone by, disappeared, the noisy troop! Now there are greyhounds in a leash, with crimson blankets, from the royal gardens where, on camp-beds, lie asleep the hunting leopards and lynxes of his Highness. Strange, lean, supple creatures, these greyhounds; very noble, with a keen light in their piercing eyes, as, with rough tongue, they lick the hand their attendant holds out to them. Not far distant I see a wedding party; fifty women, clothed in silky yellow, seated on the ground, are chanting, and the bride, a slip of a girl, ten years old, stands alone in the centre. At the end of the street, behind a grating, which makes a façade upon the side-walk, in the presence of the passing crowd, ten man-eaters, ten royal tigers, with lowered heads, measure with long, gentle steps the cage to which, after due form of law, they have been sentenced. They well deserve their title of *sahibs*, "lords," these beasts. The greatest beauty of them all is the assassin of sixteen women. I have the same feeling at sight of the formidable, gloomy head, the sinuous, gliding back, the suppleness of the thick muscles, the possible snap of the terrible jaws, the tawny splendour of the coat made of living light, that I had in Ceylon, before the sheaf of bamboos springing up into the flaming sky.

Among this multitude of images crowding one upon another, a sight which is incessantly repeated never loses its charm. You are never tired of admiring the suppleness and freshness of nude youthful figures. The slender, curving torsos of the children, both boys and girls, are adorable. The long black tresses fall over the pretty, wild, timid face, and over the delicately-modelled chest. You are conscious of the strength and health of the young muscles and the pure blood. It is something perfect. The light and shade are harmoniously blent upon the smooth bronze of the skin, all enveloped in sunshine and atmosphere. The young women, half nude, know how to adjust their drapery with extreme grace. There is nothing more delightful to the eye, more simple and tranquil, than these folds of soft stuff. In the little girls, who are extremely slender, you can see the peaceful undulation of the interior framework. They also, even the very youngest, carry upon the head handsome round jars, which they hold with stretched arms, lifted as high as possible, the chest dilated with the effort, and the bronze skin all lustrous in the sunlight.

I enter a temple whose broad steps descend into the square. Below, kneeling camels are asleep, and dogs lie upon the steps, stretched out in the sun. I ascend and enter a court, where cows wander freely over the marble pavement. In a corner are the two sacred trees, the male and female banian, the latter called the *pipala*. An old woman is running rapidly around the first one, and another woman is pouring a little water upon the leaves of the second. On one side, a second courtyard has a gallery supported by columns. There, in the shadow, a red group of seated women listen quietly to the nasal chant of a priest reading the Ramáyana. The pretty, regular faces, seen under their wraps, scarcely look absorbed in meditation. Every creature is perfectly at home in the temple : the priest seated on his heels, garlanded with flowers, swings his body to and fro to the rhythm of what he reads. Quantities of sparrows are pecking here and there, and large crows hop awkwardly upon the backs of the drowsy cows. Strictly characteristic of Hinduism is this worship in the open air, this sacred place which is at once a cow-house, an aviary, and a temple. An intense light strikes upon the walls, on which are rudely set forth in blue paint the adventures of five hundred gods. Behind the priest, at the end of the gallery, is a dark tabernacle wherein the idol is visible, a small, black-faced doll, Paravati, attired in red, and guarded by two lions. Beneath, her husband, the formidable Siva, is represented only by his emblematic stone. Here childless women come to pray, and young girls who desire to be married.

Opposite the temple, on the other side of the great square, with its seething crowd of men and beasts, stands the maharajah's college. I was admiring its façade, eccentric and rose-coloured like that of the palace of the Wind, when a student invited me to enter. I was introduced to the principal, whom I found seated in a little dark cabinet surrounded by books. A Hindu face—very gentle, refined, a little anxious-looking—the air of a student, thin, stooping, clad in a long black tunic. With quiet gestures, and in a few words of perfect English, he made me welcome, and conducted me to the class-rooms. The higher examinations being near, the students who were preparing for them had remained at home, and we saw only the pupils of the first and second year. In great pillared halls, little groups of these boys were gathered around their instructors. There were neither chairs nor benches nor desks. All rose at our entrance, and bowed low, twice touching their lips with a graceful and eager gesture. In one hall, however, the boys remained seated;

these, the principal explained to me, are the sons of the rajah and of his nobles; and, being descended from Rama and the sun, are not expected to salute a visitor.

The whole instruction here is gratuitous, and the examinations give entrance to government careers. The students are taught mathematics, the English language and literature, the dialects of India, and the Persian language. For the higher classes there is also instruction in Sanskrit, Pali, the Brahmanic, Buddhist, and Persian philosophies and the philosophies of modern Europe. Spencer and Stuart Mill are read as classics.

The principal, who is a Bengali, is ready to converse, and seems well informed as to what is going on, not only in England but in the rest of Europe. He speaks admiringly of Burnouf, of Barthélemy St. Hilaire, of Bergaigne, of the great French Sanskritists. As a rule, he says, India knows Europe only through England. "A young student who enters on the higher studies begins with the English classics : Shakespeare, Milton (a good beginning for a Hindu brain), then, and especially, Addison, Pope; later, the philosophers and economists, Locke, Hume, Adam Smith, Burke; all the thinkers of the eighteenth and nineteenth centuries, down to Herbert Spencer, whose influence is very great. In respect to France and Germany, we know them only at second hand. In general we do not know the languages of these two countries. And still we are beginning to admire something outside of England; and if

Hegel and Fichte are unfamiliar to us, we study the Oriental philosophies, especially the Upanishads, the ancient Vedantism, where we find included all Spinoza, Kant, Hegel, and Schopenhauer."

By degrees he becomes animated, and I seem to detect in him a fund of enthusiasm for the old metaphysics of his country. "Within the last five or six years," he says, "there has been a reaction in its favour. Under English influence, writers in Calcutta (the school of the Brahmos) have denounced the immoralities and follies of the Hindu religion. We now begin to recognise that under its extravagances is hidden a profound idea, and you will see that it is defended by our scholars and thinkers. We aspire to be *ourselves*. Observe the maharajah, who has introduced English ideas, has given us a college in Jaipur, a museum, and an industrial school; he does nothing against Hinduism. In his palace at Amber, there is always the sacrifice of goats to Kali. But beneath the symbol, he sees the idea; we distinguish the spirit beneath the letter, the thought contained in the religious forms which appeal to the multitude. There is a reaction against the English theism which young Bengal, that is to say, the intellectual élite of India, had welcomed with too great enthusiasm. We feel that we have something of our own, original and more profound. That we read and admire Herbert Spencer is because he criticises the idea of a personal God as one of the forms of anthropomorphism."

Does this Hindu speak truly ? Is it possible that India, becoming once more conscious of herself, is throwing off the intellectual yoke of England? Does she propose to bring forward her idea of life and the world, in opposition to the English conception? Is it possible that in the peace enjoyed under English rule, the Hindu brain, so long paralysed by Muhammadan oppression, once more begins to work? And if so, what will come of it?

Meanwhile it is interesting to see the poles of humanity thus brought face to face — English energy, practical will, and positive sense, and Hindu speculation and tendency to the metaphysical dream which makes thought triumphant, sovereign over desire and illusions, and kills the active faculties.

December 19.

A day devoted to the gratification of the eye, first, wandering alone through this astonishing pink street, filling the soul with the delight of colour, intoxicating myself with the whimsicalities of this Jaipur. Then, outside the town, we take the road leading to Amber, a pretty white ribbon, lying amid the verdure of strange thick-leaved plants, as tall as little trees. With their spiny, fat tennis-rackets of leaves, they cover the ground for a great distance; a stiff, immovable vegetation which seems that of some other planet. From the midst of it arise ancient structures, innumerable kiosks and pavilions of marble, shining in the good sunlight. Red and blue troops of men and women are gaily moving along the road.

I have never seen so many and so handsome peacocks. They wander in the road, the sapphire in their plumage gleaming softly in the light. These birds are wild, yet perfectly tame; they belong to no one, and live unmolested among the human beings. Like all harmless creatures, they are sacred to the good Hindus, who count it a religious duty to feed them. "They do no harm," Cheddy says to me soberly. "English very naughty, throw stones at them."

Farther on, a deserted palace, green with wild vegetation, seems to rest upon the mirror of a stagnant pond, whose black, infected water gives back a dull reflection. On its shore crocodiles lie motionless, asleep. All about us the graceful, sunny hills are relieved against a tranquil blue sky. The sun is not too hot, the air subtle, light, exhilarating.

Six P.M.—We make a hurried visit to the maharajah's palace, the stables where a hundred Arab horses paw the ground, the kennels, the chained elephants, the greenhouses; and then it is time to say good-bye to the pink city. Near the railway station, a little Rajput schoolboy, loaded with his Hindustani books, bids me a delicious "Good afternoon!"

In the train, at once repossessed by the European environment, one has a feeling of having come out from a brilliant theatre, from a spectacle made to amuse, to divert from real life, like one of Shakespeare's comedies, or like a pastoral of Watteau. An operetta-world, the world of a dream : this patriarchal community, these clans, these cavalcades of nobles, the children of the sun ; this wise king, beloved by his little nation, tyrannical—for instance, one may not photograph at Jaipur without the rajah's express permission—and paternal ; these warriors, with lance and shield, with their whimsical beards and showy dress ; the happy, laughing people ; the blue dogs, the hunting leopards and lynxes. It is the stage-scene of an operetta, these streets crushed-strawberry colour, the pink houses which you cannot believe are really stone, the crenellated castles on the hills, the light, fantastic structures, the palace of the Wind, the palace of the Clouds, the gate of Rubies, the hall of Splendours, the humid greenhouses full of a fresh odour of vaporous ferns, the fields covered with thick-leaved plants, the blue peacocks popping out from thickets, the deserted kiosks on the shore of dark pools. It is an operetta-existence where nothing is serious, or heavy, or sad, that is lived by this laughing, artist-population, who do no other work than carve little gods and little beasts in marble, embroider slippers with silver, illuminate their walls with blue designs, bestride Arab horses, feed the birds of the air, fly kites, and enjoy in full security the light of day and the goodness of things. Yes, a happy, simplified, childish life, which lacks only its orchestra, chorus, and ballet, and whose dazzling poetic vision clings in one's memory, as he turns away toward the darkness and the sadness of our Europe.

The hills have closed in about the charming city. Now a golden dust floats in the air. A solitary heron stands motionless on the edge of a lake, which is all rose-colour and blue in the twilight radiance.

CHAPTER VIII

BOMBAY

December 21.

THIRTY-SIX hours of railway. As we advance southward, toward the great English city, the train becomes crowded: fat babus, important native merchants, encumber the carriages with their travelling-bags, loll indolently and insolently upon the cushions. The third-class are crammed with a Hindu crowd, chattering, laughing, and conversing. For luggage they have only their brass jars, engraved with figures of Krishna and Ganesa. At the stations Brahmans, loaded with leathern bottles, come to refill these jars. Only the Brahmans can perform this duty, for a Kshatriya travelling would be defiled by drinking water which a Sudra had poured out. But everybody can touch what the Brahman has touched. Be his duties ever so servile, the Brahman remains a Brahman, preserving his supernatural virtue; the superiority of caste remains, whatever the inferiority of occupation.

There is little to notice. In these long journeys the mind, blurred by the multitude of images lately perceived, becomes somnolent, and is interested in nothing. Cities rapidly seen, Baroda,

Ahmedabad, great railway stations, tiffins, breakfasts with the everlasting curry, the simple outlines of blue mountains. Athwart all this, the same arid country; and, perpetually, the amazing troops of monkeys leaping in the tall brush.

The second morning, as I awake, there is a surprise. Suddenly you seem to be in Ceylon again. Again the moist region, hot, stormy; the great equatorial vegetation. Everywhere there is water. Dense forests of palm-trees descend toward lagoons, mirror their slender colonnades in the blue estuaries, and their great green leafy coronets, rising in the moist air, make shadowy arches, under which small houses find shelter. The ground is black, marshy, abounding in pools of water. Thousands of large-footed birds people the edges of the marshes and of the salt-water inlets. Here and there, on the west, the water is continuous; roads form and increase in extent, immense spaces of a calm and splendid blue, spotted with islets that seem half-sunken forests, and bordered here with cocoanut groves, there with low hills, which their dense vegetation covers like a thick bluish mist. Now, a great space of the Indian Ocean appears; the space seems to broaden to contain all this light.

Then a clattering of iron; a great uproar; a huge railway terminus; we come into the station of Bori-Bunder; this is Bombay.

Five P.M.—It is extremely warm, with a moist heat as of a greenhouse, very fatiguing and enervating. One has not strength to select and group impressions, and, indeed, it is all too varied. This city is composed of several cities, spread out over five islands. It would seem that all the races, all the religions, all the forms of architecture, all the industries of the globe are blended and confused here into an extraordinary mixture, seething and smoking in the sunlight.

I am sitting on the terrace of a café on the Esplanade. Here, the island is contracted into a very narrow tongue of land, the sea visible on both sides, on the right a great harbour, girt with forests on the remote edge; on the left a broad yellow beach which, curving slightly, stretches away toward a promontory, and dark, shiny clumps of palm-trees. Upon this beach, two miles or so of straight road, which is bordered on the left by immense buildings, Gothic or Venetian, separated from the city by lawns and gardens.

Along this road by the sea, all the commercial aristocracy of Bombay is now on its way to the Esplanade to enjoy the evening breeze. Here, facing the harbour, the carriages are standing in a crowd, while the Sepoy band plays European airs. Beside the fat Hindus in their white tunics and pink turbans, many Englishmen and Parsis, the latter dressed in European style, but grotesquely coiffed with a mitre of starred pasteboard; also, European and native officers are gathered outside the cafés, sipping their lemonade or cocktails. There are, moreover, many ayahs, Hindu nurses with their babies, adorned like shrines covered with velvet and brocade.

In the carriages, motionless as at a race, the Parsi ladies sit in state. This is the first glimpse of feminine "society" in India. The high-caste Hindu women are all mysteriously shut up in the *zenanas*, and you must go to the dealers to see the silks and costly embroideries of Benares and Delhi. But here they may be seen in the open air and sunlight, draped about the supple and living figure : yonder old lady is clad in one piece of material which enwraps her from head to foot; but the material is a heavy crimson silk, fringed with gold. As she moves slightly, it falls in great lustrous folds. They are all thus attired, in Greek style, and have veils of muslin, or of mauve or blue silk, which follow the pure outline of the head, and with their strong, simple colour set off the gentleness of Aryan features and the whiteness of soft faces. Languid, leaning far back in their carriages, they await, these opulent Oriental women, with half-closed eyelids, the evening breeze which shall reanimate them.

And there is a marvellous light upon this showy assemblage, a light of a kind that one never observes except in the neighbourhood of great spaces of tropical seas, coming from the water, as well as from the sky. I have seen nothing like the sky here, either in Egypt, Ceylon, or the interior of India. It is not at all blue, but is all white, liquid light, full of heat and moisture.

Now the sun sinks behind Malabar Hill, and in this air, peculiar to Bombay, there are very curious effects of radiation. A rose-coloured vapour invades everything, encircles sea and land, and covers the remote forests, which are not relieved against the golden horizon, but vanish into it and disappear. The sun seems to melt as it sinks, and to sink in front of the trees.

Soon a light breeze springs up, and the roseate water quivers. The great black steamers in a row seem dead things in this universal faint stir. Out toward the open sea, clouds of vessels have spread their wings, and in the silence and the light fly like a dream, so tranquil that they seem to be borne away upon some broad current, as if the whole water were slipping away with them; and in following them you forget the Sepoy band, and the parti-coloured ground, and the languid Parsi ladies, until the little pink swarm is so far, so far away that it seems to be going out of our world, to be rising into space, into those blessed regions where is nothing but the calm of ether.

December 23.

Certainly it is not easy to describe the aspect of this Bombay, diverse and confused as it is. The eye cannot arrange in order the images which fill it. I write them at random, as they recur this evening after a day spent in the streets. Perhaps this is the only way to give an idea of the whirl of forms and colours, the confusion of races and of religions.

Everywhere, and at every hour of the day, there is the streaming crowd, more dense than in Benares, a motley crowd wherein are blended all the costumes of Asia; wherein all types of humanity elbow one another; Europeans in coats, the Arab with his fez, Persians, Afghans, thick-lipped negroes, slender Malays, effeminate Cinhalese, Parsis and Jews, Chinese in robes of silk. Probably, since the time of Alexander, there has been no such epitome of the entire world, no city so cosmopolitan. There are bits of London here, bits of Benares, bits of Shanghai. Underneath this flux of foreign races, there is a native substratum of half-naked humanity: fakirs grey with ashes; letter-writers kneeling on the side-walk; schools receiving instruction in the open air; worshippers bending before sacred images, covering them with native flowers; coolies who run, balancing packages at the end of a long bamboo; naked barbers who are shaving their customers; a whole population of women who serve as porters, girls of low caste, almost negresses, dripping with sweat, their legs bare to the thigh, sitting on the ground in the shade of the walls, a crowd of them together, miserable-looking objects, stupefied by hard labour; and over everything an atmosphere loaded with vapour.

I see ancient carts dragged by heavy, patient oxen, amid tram-cars, victorias, palanquins, sedan-chairs. I see walls covered with blue elephants, with placards, in English, Persian, Urdu, Hindustani; mosques, Christian churches, — Anglican, Wesleyan, Catholic,—Hindu temples, Parsi temples. Railways run along the boulevards, past pagodas bristling with their hundred thousand monsters, past the statue of Her Majesty the Queen, past the

Gothic buildings of the University, past the blue expanse where sleep at anchor the great steamships.

From this mass of images repeated all day long, melting one into another, I essay to detach a few salient pictures. Here is the great market, six o'clock in the morning; in a fog, shot through with sunlight, three or four thousand men, women, children, naked or clad in beautiful colours, struggle with each other among the oranges, bananas, pine-apples, flowers, amid a deafening clamour which rises from cages of monkeys and baskets of birds; and, before soft heaps of silvery fish, there are rows of half-nude women with lustrous dark skins, kneeling upon tables. Here are the offices of the railway station at Bori-Bunder, an immense hall, where two hundred employés, leaning over their desks, are blackening paper; or, pen over ear, are searching registers. It might be a great banking house or a public office in Paris; but these men are all Hindus, all worshippers of Siva and Vishnu, marked on the forehead with the religious sign, the three lines drawn with ashes. There is the sea, visible at every street corner, blue, motionless, as in a painted picture. There is the native city—a city in a forest, a crowd of narrow, tortuous streets, under an uninterrupted roof of palms. There is a little street, where a marriage festivity is in progress, crowded with half-clad humanity, which flows slowly like a glutinous wave among the sumptuous crowd of guests whose silk garments are richly lustrous. There are rows and rows of little girls, draped in splendid stuffs, and these small dark faces, with smooth, lustrous bands of hair, so black that it has a blue gleam like a raven's wing, are strangely grave and childish. The crimson and orange of the sinuous satins flame against a whitish background of smooth limbs and fat torsos of Brahmans, and against innumerable nude figures. And all this crowd makes an eddy in the narrow street, sending out a suffocating heat under the palm-trees which shelter the houses, and the sacred fig-trees, where squirrels run and parrots chatter, as many as the figs.

At the end of this Hindu city, near the sea, is the hospital for animals. There are kennels of mangy dogs; one very feeble old eagle; some pigeons and parrots; peacocks dragging through the courts the splendours of their tails; a consumptive porcupine whose dull eyes are pitiful to see; a small crippled deer; and halls filled with blind cows. Through this curious menagerie wander idly many Brahmans, perpetually chewing betel, and living as brothers among these sufferers, these animals who are sacred because they manifest for an instant Siva the Indestructible, because they are sparks in the vibrating flame of life. "Health, O cow!" says a powerful *mantra*, "thou mother of Rudra, sister of Aditrya, source of Ambrosia!"

Returning through the broad streets of the business town, you observe a very curious blending of English and Hindu life. Great walls are covered with placards like these: "Theistic Bombay

Temporary Relief Association." "Hindu Cricket Club." "Parsee Cricket Association." I should like to see a game played by these Orientals. They would scarcely put much ardour into their game, the Hindu cricket-players. Clubs of native "sportsmen" are quite the most amusing copy of England that I have seen in India, more comic even than an article on English morals signed by a babu. Very English also, this union of a theistic society and a cricket club—a compound of athletics and philanthropy. Probably the cricket-players are theists, and the theists are cricket-players. Similarly, in a London shop, I saw the photograph of an Anglican bishop with this note appended: "One of the Oxford Eight, in the University race of 18—." In England this exploit completes an episcopal personality as much as would an edition of Euripides or a volume of sermons. Everybody has heard of an ideal type, the "muscular Christian."

Elsewhere, red flags are flying above the heads of a Hindu crowd. "Hallelujah!" say the flags. "Are you saved? Are you fighting? If not, why not? When do you intend to get saved?" Sandwich-men are going about announcing "the arrival of the Salvation Army from Canada, and a general attack upon the Devil by Captain Hallelujah Smith, formerly a circus clown." In the midst of the Hindu crowd, the English Salvationists form a little ring: they are all barefooted, clad in Oriental costume, the women draped in red, their blonde faces surrounded with orange muslin, the men in Bedouin mantles and turbans. Curious, these English faces, the soft pink and white skin, in Asiatic costumes!

A kind of little Hindu monkey makes a confession in a nasal voice. Then, successively, the English Salvationists testify, each holding an umbrella as parasol. Then a drum, castanets, and a key-bugle. The Englishwomen stand quietly, their hands drooping and clasped, and sing hymns to polka tunes, while the men accompany with accordions. One of them makes an exhortation in Hindustani, a very young girl, in Oriental drapery, her bare feet in the dust, the eyes of an angel, a lily complexion untouched by the Indian sun, a pensive expression, so serious, calm, and maidenly, one of Burne-Jones's Madonnas.

There is something at once comic and touching in the energy and sincerity of these evangelists. Their great lack is of that sympathetic imagination which makes it possible to conceive modes of soul foreign to one's self. How much superior were the Jesuits who, in the eighteenth century, had such success in China! With what skill they adapted Christianity to the faculties and needs of the Chinese soul! These people here employ the same procedure to touch the heart of a poor day-labourer in the East End, moving about in the black mud, the stinging fog of the Docks, and to reach these Hindu souls—of which we are so ignorant! The grand Wesleyan hymns sung to tunes from the dance hall, what emotion can they awaken in these Asiatics? Are they touched at sight of young women who have come so far, to mingle with the Bombay populace, to wear the same clothes, to live the same life with them, to be their sisters, to love them in Jesus Christ?

On this point, Cheddy Lal, whom I have consulted, says: "The other missionaries are liked better. These do not come in a carriage, as Europeans should; they dress as we do; they are thought to be poor, and they are despised."

I returned by the beach, which is not on the edge of the harbour, but of the open sea. Not a boat to be seen. From here the city is hidden, and there is only this yellow sand, wet from the retiring tide, and the soft blue of the ocean. There are familiar perfumes of seaweed inhaled, in childhood, on Breton sands. Inland, there must be great cliffs, sombre ridges of moorland, lighted by pale yellow broom. This landscape, the same in Europe and in India, tranquillises the mind, discomposed at sight of great ethnic differences, this seething mass of foreign peoples.

Little waves are running in; they rise with a pale transparency, tremble in a silvery gleam and break with a soft splash. A Parsi has come down to the edge of the water, and, his lips moving in prayer, watches the sun, whose throbbing disk is about to disappear. Just as it touches the water-line, the Parsi bends his head twice, and then stretches out his arms toward the great rosy radiance which floats in the west.

December 24.

This morning, after the *chota hazri*, I went up to Malabar Hill, a green promontory covered with villas and palm-trees; between them is seen the vague, shining blue of the sea, and the sparkle of charming, misty Bombay. The morning dew is evaporating in a thin mist whose white veils float, waver, are torn like gauze, and out of which the tall, fresh palms lift their heads. On the ground are flowers, as in Ceylon, flowers of azure and crimson, on which tremble big drops of water.

Farther on, a garden where this vegetation is growing regularly with a studied order; a garden like that of the Taj, solemn in its light and silence and beauty. Among the clumps of trees rise three towers, white, low, extremely massive, that are not temples, or habitations of man, enigmatic, disturbing here in the solitude. Around, great birds hover in the air.

It is the Parsi cemetery; this garden is a funereal spot; upon these towers the dead are exposed and are devoured by vultures; a priest came to explain these things to me.

Clothed in white, he says, two by two, each couple holding the two ends of a muslin scarf in token of their common grief, through the streets of Bombay, along the shore, under the palm-trees, among the flower-beds, the Parsis slowly follow their dead, whom two bearers carry, wrapped in a shroud. When they reach the foot of the tower, a little door opens, the body is received, and the door closed again. Then the procession disperses. No man has ever seen what takes place behind the closed door, except the two mysterious guardians of the cemetery.

The platform on the summit of the tower is divided into three concentric zones, inclined toward a central well which communicates with a vault. The dead are laid in these great circles, the men, the women, the children. Each body is taken from its shroud, for, says a text of the Zend Avesta: "Naked thou camest into the world, and naked shalt thou go out from it."

At ten o'clock in the morning, and at six in the evening, the great tawny vultures come flying from all the points of the sky, and take up their position upon the towers. In less than fifteen minutes not a trace of the human form is left except a skeleton, which the extreme heat of the sun soon separates, and the rain carries down into the well. Here at the bottom, where the dust and *débris* accumulate, there are filtering stones, which purify the rain water, so that no human particle enters the ground. Saith the Zend Avesta: "Thou shalt not defile the earth, thy mother."

As we stood in the garden more than fifty vultures were sitting gravely on the edge of a tower, and I could plainly see their strange, fierce eyes, those fixed eyes where shines a flame fed on human fuel. An admirable sepulchre, those birds' bodies! No sooner dead than to live again, to return at once into a whirl of life, more rapid and brilliant by far than the preceding. To have been a poor Parsi *grande dame*, one of those languid women, in her sumptuous drapery, waiting indolently for a breath of air to come, and now to cleave the glowing sky, with impetuous, strident flight !

Around us, the calm and splendour of the tropical garden. The warm air is full of perfumes, and the perpetual little striped squirrels run merrily through the avenues.

From here the view over the city is very beautiful. The sea is of a very soft, dull blue, under the sky white with its heat, vaporous, pale by reason of the moisture which it draws up. At the left, on the shore of this water, is another sea of dark and lustrous green, whose waves are motionless, a sea of palm-trees, out of which rise turrets and Gothic belfries and roofs of pagodas. This world is beautiful.

CHAPTER IX

ELURA

December 26.

NEARLY two hundred miles on the Great Peninsular by moonlight, among weird silhouettes of mountains rising in vast flocks. Forests, houses, cliffs, all the details of the landscape disappear, and the great silent shapes, misty as phantoms under the pallid moon, seem the sole inhabitants of the dark globe. Then thirteen hours in a cart, over a bad road, along with the driver, in the Nizam, in the heart of the Dekkan—this may well have tranquillised one's mind, after the heat and uproar of Bombay.

A savage deserted country, carpeted with moorland and jungle. Sometimes a little Hindu hamlet, a small pyramidal pagoda, grotesque, complicated, like all pagodas, and a sacred pool where the peasants bathe in the morning, according to the ceremonial.

Upon the road, not a person, except, about nine o'clock, a troop of men, children, women, following a string of heavy, antique wains drawn by big white oxen. Whither are they going? It looks like the migration of a tribe, after the most primitive fashion.

This nomad horde is soon out of sight. About

noon, southward, is outlined against the sky a tawny line of hills. It is a vast amphitheatre opening into a great plain, lying north and south, pierced with caves by the men of earlier times. Here, in the heart of the peninsula, are the silent haunts of the divinities who, for three thousand years, have succeeded each other in this Indian land. There sit the Vedic gods, Indra and Surya ; then, the inert Buddhas, with closed eyes and crossed legs ; and then, the Brahmanic Pantheon— Siva, Paravati, Vishnu, and the whole train of their incarnations ; then, the twenty-four Sages of the Jains ; all hewn in the ancient rock, cut out in the mountain of which they still remain a part, alone in the solitude, in face of the unchanging landscape ; intact as on the first day.

At twenty rods' distance from the mountain, nothing is distinguishable. All is covered with a forest of impenetrable brushwood, the sombre jungle which seems thrown down from the hill-top to guard the secret of the place. It grows in the glowing sand in the dry and terrible heat, all in a mass at the foot of the cliff. There are no flowers here, none of the luxuriance and beauty of the vegetation of Ceylon or Bombay. All is arid and burning. We advance cautiously. Under the thorny shrubs, upon the glowing mica, gleams the gliding of formidable cobras. They debar access to the temples of Siva ; and one remembers that, in images of the god, they are multiplied around his neck and his waist, mystic symbols of alldestroying Time.

We reach the foot of the cliff, which rises a perpendicular wall. Just in front of us, it yawns apart, disclosing within an isolated grey mass of rock about as high as the cliff itself; but there is something peculiar about this mass of rock: it is hollowed out, recessed, its surface is rough with scales and little spires, like a granite cliff tortured by the eternal gnawing of the sea. Suddenly you recognise the entangled lines of a pagoda. This is the Kailasa, "the Paradise" of Siva, a Hindu temple made of a piece of the mountain: pavilions, terraces, pyramids, bell-towers, stairs, obelisks, guardian elephants, all out of one block, all hewn in one enormous stone, which has been detached, cut out, chased, like a piece of ivory in the hands of a Chinese workman. On each side and behind it, like the case to contain a precious object, three rough, perpendicular walls of rock rise to the height of more than a hundred feet, as if hewn by three strokes of a magic sword, to isolate the rock which glorifies Siva. The open space where the Kailasa stands is two hundred and seventy-six feet in length, with an average breadth of a hundred and fifty-four feet; the nearly isolated rocky mass itself is a hundred and sixty-four feet long, a hundred and nine broad at its widest, and rises to a height of ninety-six feet.

As you stand looking at this Kailasa, a strange feeling comes over you, at first entirely inexplicable. Is it because of the surrounding silence and desert; is it because there is nothing constructed in this pagoda—I mean to say, no stone laid upon stone;

or is it because the uniform tone of colouring is that of rock weathered since the beginning of the geologic epochs, that of the brown wall, which from north to south, as far as the eye can see, bounds the plain ? One cannot say, but the singular fact remains that nothing here suggests the idea of human labour. There is no inscription, no detail suggesting a daily ceremonial, no place where the priests could be lodged. This is a work of Nature, in praise of the divinity who symbolised her; this pagoda, which makes part of the solid strata of the earth, is like an eternal, indestructible thing—not, however, inert, but still alive with the life of the great earth itself. For its roof of massive rock is still covered with all the primitive stratum of vegetable growth, bristling with grasses and with great stiff plants which seem to be sacred candelabra. All around, the heated atmosphere quivers in white waves, and animal life palpitates: flocks of parrots whirling in the air like green flames; crows hopping over the ancient statues; squirrels, which seem at home here, running over the steps, trotting in and out through the tabernacles. Inside the Kailasa, in the darkness of the sanctuaries dug into the living rock, in the mysterious bare chambers with their mystic symbols of Siva, bats fly in silent circles.

I walk around outside the monolith, and am overwhelmed by the enormous size of the stone box in which it stands, of the wall which shuts it in and overhangs it, recessed at its base, hewn out in a black groove, a sombre gallery going entirely around it, and supported by rough pillars. Above this gallery, the cliff drops plumb, like a heavy, voluminous mantle of rock, striated with blue lines by the eternal drip of water. On the three sides, facing this perfectly naked cliff, the Kailasa presents its tangle of figures of gods and animals; it lifts its pyramids, it unfolds all its complication of outlines. There could be nothing so impressive as the contrast: remove this pagoda out of the brute mass from which it was hewn, set it up in the open air, and you would lose the feeling of the blind, crushing labour which separated it from the cliff, in order to carve it. Especially, you would detach it from nature; it would no longer be a part of the earth itself, thus expressing the fundamental idea of the Siva-worship.

The power, the constant energy, itself invariable amid the motion or the pause of its dispersed manifestations, the Being, unknowable and absolute, who displays himself in the incessant production of individual beings, from whom comes, into whom is absorbed all life, could by no symbol be so well expressed as by this rock which, rising out of the solid strata that form the substance of the globe, elsewhere crops out in cliffs, but here follows geometric lines of terraces; then becomes supple, complicated, undulating, in organic forms: represents all manifestations of life: first, an army of gigantic elephants, almost completely detached from the rock, but still making part of the brute mass; then, higher up, among entanglements of tropical creepers, among processions of monkeys and of tigers, rises, yet still caught at its sides, in the animal world; displays after this, human forms, unfolds the epic of the Ramàyana, relates the conquest of the inferior races by the nobler races ; higher still, multiplies figures of genii and secondary gods ; then is excavated in mysterious halls where, in the darkness, centre and root of all this flowering of life upon the outer walls, is the mystic symbol of Siva ; and, at last, slender, light, airy, lifts its sharp, pyramidal point into radiant space.

Right and left, as we leave the Kailasa, there are sacred caves piercing the side of the hill, along a length of nearly two miles.

First are Sivaist crypts, difficult of access, invisible from without. We are obliged to cling to projections of the cliff, and creep over masses of *débris* bound tight by the jungle to the face of the rock. These caves are the secret places where the old Brahmins concealed their religious mysteries, and he who penetrated here ignorant, would indeed emerge initiated.

Deep galleries lead into the hillside, made visible at first by a wan, cold light, which lies pallid on the grey stone; then plunging into an ever-deepening darkness, between rough pillars hewn out of the rock. In this darkness, where there is no sound but the rush of bats, you see gleaming eyes of gold in giant bas-reliefs of monstrous gods, dancing or sitting enthroned. The farther you advance, the more indistinct becomes this row of forms, at first visible in the grey light from the mouth of the cave, but all the time growing fainter, until they are lost in the distant darkness. Why are they all so much alike ; why have they all the same attributes ? This is Siva, in the entire series of his incarnations. Yes ; all these mystic outlines, sinuous and flexible as life, are those of his various bodies; and each of these huge bas-reliefs has one of the god's faces.

Here he is, Siva, the Destroyer, and his three eyes, which behold the past, the present, the future, shine with a white light, that light which reduces all creatures to ashes ; his six arms brandish swords, whereon hang transpierced corpses, his feet trample upon skeletons. Elsewhere, he reposes, contemplative, girt with serpents about his neck and body, emblems of his eternity. Again, Siva, with soft, confused outlines, mysterious, androgynous, smiling. From his side emerges a soft-outlined female figure, and above his head, very faint, in much lower relief than the figure, a cloud of human forms rise, floating, as the smoke ascends from a flame. It is still Siva, who, far back in the dark gallery, smiles at Paravati ; it is he who dances merrily, surrounded by his buffoons; it is he who, again, fierce, with teeth set in fury, transpierces a child. And skeletons, signifying death, alternate with bulls, which signify life. And in the depths of the gallery a nude stone represents the eternal Siva emblem.

Before all this transparency of symbol, this revelation of the god, one stands astonished. The idea radiates from these images and transfigures them. This Siva is no longer a foreign divinity, peculiar to a certain race and a certain epoch, to be observed and studied as such. We know this power, ourselves. It is Nature expressed in these changeful forms, outlined here on the walls in this subterranean solitude. This is the divinity manifested as well in the perpetual coming forth of young and brilliant life, as in its frightful destruction; the eternal and impassive, who knows not the suffering nor the joy of the created. The Brahmanic religion conceived the destroying and the renewing force as two aspects of the same power; it made of the Destroyer and the Regenerator one divinity; and in this lies its great originality.

While other races, powerless to rise above the human point of view, regarded good and evil, the beautiful and the hideous, as distinguishing attributes, and classed their gods in accordance with characteristics strictly relative to human sensibilities, the Hindus conceived that, from the eternal point of view, there was neither god nor devil, but an absolute Power which, whether creating or destroying, remains itself the same. More definitely, death appeared to them as one of the changes whose succession makes a life. For, according to them, as according to modern science,—*La vie, c'est la mort*, says Claude Bernard, —the living being is but a form, a mode of grouping; its material is for ever passing away; we live by the periodic death of the cellules whose association makes our body. We are eddies, at every moment composed of new substance; as each eddy gives up a certain quantity of matter, it absorbs and carries off a certain other quantity of matter, equivalent to what it has lost; and deaths are perpetually made good by births.

It is the same with all the groups everywhere in the visible world, they are forming or separating, but separating only to form new combinations, under whose variety persists a diffused being, itself one and imperishable. The world may be compared to an ocean, in which are moving millions of waves. Each wave which rises and sinks is a life which begins and ends, no sooner falling in foam than an irresistible impulse lifts it again toward the light. But who does not see that these rythmic undulations are only appearances, since at each moment their material is different and in each one of them there is nothing real except the single, general force, which blindly, indifferently, without regard for local shocks or interferences, keeps all this sea in its murmurous motion? An individual being is but a momentary fragment of this force. The individual changes, grows, dies; but the force remains unaffected. It is the same Siva, radiant in the candid young forehead of the girl, in her firm delicate cheek with its tint of rose, who reduces to nameless liquids this corpse upon which we dare not look. It is the same Siva who acted in our primitive nebula, and who now is sun and planets, and the continents, seas, mountains of the globe, its organic forms, its races of men, its communities and cities.

It is the same Siva who, transforming visible action into molecular, by the slow destruction of planets, returns to his primitive condition of abstract energy, whence may emerge a new sun, planets, seas, continents, vegetation, a whole multiple and luminous life.

Let us go further: this energy of our solar system, even, is not an isolated power; it is but part of the total energy, since throughout the universe, all stars—or, to speak more exactly, all particles of matter—make their attraction felt. Our system moves, as a whole, toward a certain point in the firmament. Who knows if it is not describing an immense circle, lessening slowly; if it may not fall, and all the other systems also, into a certain central point, as its own planets fall into its sun, and if the whole universe does not tend to return to homogeneity, to the *undifferentiated?* This possible law Hindu wisdom may have grasped, in speaking of those " days of Brahma," those incalculable periods, during which the neuter Bráhmă expands, develops, throws out beings, attains consciousness, contracts again, returns into its primitive condition; becomes again the neuter Bráhmă. Had not the Sivaist this idea, in saying that, at the end of each *kalpa*, Siva destroys men, gods, demons, all created things?

Whether or not science, at the present day, considers probable these alternations of development and of universal dissolution, certainly she makes known to us a universal and permanent power, acting at every moment, and at every point of the universe, and of which we can say nothing except that it manifests itself to us above and below, in the general and the special, in movements, in cycles of organisations and dissolutions, in phenomena of local groupings and of separations of matter, which are each other's complement, appearing, according to the point of view, as lives or deaths, as ends or beginnings. How better personify this power than as the Hindus have done? How better represent it than by this Siva whom they call "the Destroyer-Organiser"—"he who brings life out of death?"

In a sacred picture which I found at Jaipur, he is seated at the bottom of a cave, in the depths of the earth. Above him is a rich country, luxuriant in vegetation. His beautiful feminine limbs repose inert: his serene lips are parted in a mysterious smile. Upon his forehead the crescent of the new moon measures time; around his neck a snake signifies the endless revolutions of the years; other serpents, entwined about his loins, tell of the circle of births and deaths. His braided hair supports the fruitful Ganges; his trident announces his triple power—to create, to destroy, to re-create. He holds a bow, a thunderbolt, and an axe, the weapons surmounted by skulls. A bull sleeps at his feet. All these symbols are here in these carvings of Elura. He is the reproductive force, "the eternally blest," with its emblem, the mystic stone; he is the power which dissolves, symbolised by skeletons and swords; he is "the great ascetic," passionless, immovable, immutable, "rooted in the same place for millions of years." He is the god of Brahmans, of grammarians, of scholars; that is to say, he is intellect, order, language. He is the lord of the dance and wine; that is, of gay and brilliant life. He is bi-sexed; and vaguely-outlined figures rise about him in vaporous processions.

In the obscure depths of the hill, upon the rude walls of rock, one grasps the meaning of these images left there for all time—far from cities, far from the tumult of human life—by men hidden from us in the darkness of the past, of whom we know absolutely nothing except that they were the contemporaries of our barbaric ancestors, and that they lived at this point in space. But him whom they perceived behind all things, we, to-day, also perceive; we hear him also; in our "Faust" we hear his voice:

"In the stream of life, in the whirl of action, I float, I rise, I sink, I move hither and thither. Births and tombs, eternal sea, changeful motion, ardent life; I work at the noisy loom of time and weave the mantle of divinity."

All the religious history of India is concealed in these caves of Elura. There is a succession of Sivaist halls, overloaded with the same wealth of sculptures and bas-reliefs.

Here is a very unadorned cave sunk far into the rock, supported by rude pillars whose sole ornament is a symbolic circle. The walls are rough-hewn, and it would seem that this sanctuary was left unfinished. As we advance the light from the entrance grows faint, and it is all blackness before us. We are about to turn away, with the idea that there is nothing to see, when I become aware of a huge phantom somewhere in the distance, an apparition which nails me to the spot. My eyes have become accustomed to the darkness; and there, a hundred and twenty feet from the cave's mouth, a giant figure, a white, colossal Buddha, seated with crossed hands, a smile frozen on the lips, formidable in its rigidity, is vaguely outlined, at the very end of the cave, against the blackness of a niche. This is all; he sits alone in the darkness, in this silence as of a tomb; in this great excavation, hewn out of the rock, remote from all outside life. At his feet a pool of black water, motionless like himself, reflects his smile and his immobility.

There are several caves like this, occupied by solitary Buddhas, who, with half-closed eyes, have entered into serenity. A strange contrast with the Sivaist caves, overflowing with all forms of life, expressive of all the exuberance of the Hindu imagination. Yet, notwithstanding their difference, they translate conceptions which are each other's complement. Those lead to this, as an orgy of metaphysical speculation leads to the paralysis of the will and complete inaction, as his meditation upon the one Existence has led the Brahman to forget his own personal being, and—showing him illusions everywhere and destroying desire within him—has set him free from all temptation to effort or action. Siva and Buddha sit side by side, as Brahmanism and Buddhism have been able to live in harmony, one appealing to the mental powers, the other dictating the practical life; and these caves may have been contemporary. At the same time, the extreme difference of the styles would seem to indicate that long spaces of time separate them, and that the hill remains sacred to successive cults, not merely to the Sivaists and Buddhists, but also to the Jains, who have in their turn excavated sanctuaries in these cliffs; and that all the Indian religions, one after another, have inscribed themselves here.

They may pass, and reappear; and the races themselves may vanish; but the Buddha will never relax his smile—this smile which has been upon his lips for two thousand years. How peaceful the cool darkness of the cave, at the feet of the great tranquil figure! What happiness it must be to feel one's self at last enfranchised; to be no longer conscious of the flight of life, of the incessant fall into the sad past of all beloved objects; to conquer time as he has done whom twenty centuries leave untouched! As I stand leaning against his solid knee, under the deathless gesture of his wan hand, I can see the calm gaze which has filtered between his eyelids ever since the day when a nation of labourers—vanished how long ago—detached him from the rock. Out there, at the other end of the gallery, there is daylight, a luminous rectangle, framed in the sombre stone, and cut by black columns; there is a far-off, splendid landscape, a vast country, quivering in the overheated air. Flocks of birds make a streak across the torrid sky. In the distance glitters a small pagoda, dominating a hamlet where, for many a year, lives of men have silently followed one another.

CHAPTER X

THE VOYAGE

December 28.

AT seven in the morning we leave Bombay. You go on board the steamer, select your cabin, study the faces of the people with whom you are to spend the next three weeks, go to look at the engine—and suddenly become aware that you are off. In the blue of the water, a great, rigid white furrow—broad as a road, whispering and pulsating—leads back to the already misty hillsides and the glittering roofs half hidden by trees. The watery space rapidly increases behind us; all the low ground soon vanishes. Only the mountains long remain visible, as on any remote shore.

It is always sad, this sudden disappearance of a world in which one has lived for some time. Abruptly these things, which just now were present, enter into the past, and take on the halo of an inexpressible regret for that which is no more. These memories—at present a part of one's self —are destined to lose their colour; the feeling which now accompanies them will let them go; presently, they will die: and you feel a great indifference—it would be a great aversion, if these memories were more dear—for this future self, this stranger, who will be composed of sentiments at this moment unknown. The Buddha was right in teaching that grief comes of time.

All passes away with marvellous rapidity; this ocean, this sun casting the shadow of the rigging, this ship, seem to be the only realities. It is difficult to conceive clearly that there is a pink Jaipur, a real city of solid structures, or a seething Benares upon which this light is shining.

With what facility one returns into the native environment! European things recover their hold upon you so rapidly that you seem never to have left them. Almost immediately it becomes amusing to observe one's fellow-travellers. There are a dozen, differing widely from each other, whose lives are thrown together here for a few days. The perpetual contact establishes intimacy so complete that we soon seem to have known each other always. There are no reserves; after five days one has more "human documents" than after a season of balls and dinners in Paris.

Here is an Englishman, an officer of hussars. I attempt to describe him, because he seems to me a specimen of a very important class. Twenty-six years old: "a splendid young fellow." Fair and freckled, with clear-cut features; his blue eyes brilliant, straightforward, bold, and kind; a happy face, lighted with rapid smiles; sometimes, abruptly, a great burst of laughter. You can see the enthusiasm of youth, high spirits, the constant joy of a free and generous existence. In the afternoon he pitches quoits with the ardour and vivacity of a boy. He puts his heart into the game, and his movements show the suppleness of the fresh young figure. In repose, he has the alert and simple bearing of a man perfectly at his ease, master of himself, habituated to independence, with a reserve of gravity under the sparkle of animal spirits.

His young wife admires him as Desdemona, Othello: to her he is the steadfast, strong, and faithful man, who is the young English girl's ideal, the hero of all the English novels. And indeed there is in him a grave and solid substratum of character. Upon religion and duty, and the family relations, he is endowed with hereditary ideas, extremely well defined and deeply rooted. Physically and morally he is a "gentleman," by race and education. "My ancestors," he says, with a certain pride, "came into Ireland with Cromwell." Born upon the paternal estate, he is the heir of a line of "squires."

His first years of childhood, spent in the country among the farmers who loved and respected him as "the young master"; the generous home life in the great manor-house; the first riding to hounds, with his father and grandfather, they in red coats on their big hunters, he mounted on a little pony; the study of the Bible, and the firm fixing of religious sentiment, from the nursery, by pictures, by texts which decorate the walls, by family prayers, where all the servants are also present, by long and solemn services, listened to in "the squire's pew" of the parish church. Then Rugby, the sense of freedom and self-respect acquired, the contact with "the other boys," whose good opinion must be gained; much cricket and football. After this, preparation for the army examinations, the military career having been chosen as most worthy of "a gentleman." He is now lieutenant in "a crack regiment," and speaks proudly of his corps: "My regiment was at the battle of Quatre-Bras. Three times they charged the Poles, but without being able to reach them. Every one of the officers was killed. We have the whole story of it in the regimental *Gazette*."

In India his life had three great interests: his wife (with whom he is in love), the service, and sport. A liberal, expensive life: that of a gentleman among his equals. I saw the photograph of his house, a great airy villa, with Doric columns, standing in a broad lawn; his wife in an English cart, before the portico. "You can't be an officer," he explains, "without resources of your own." His pay is a hundred and seventy-five rupees a month. The mess table alone, with wine, costs two hundred. Horses and uniforms are expensive; the club, the dinners, are costly. In short, they live as aristocrats, as nobles; and in general they are nobles, in pride and courage. A noble's duty is to be a leader; and these sons of squires are well fitted to lead. The sentiment of duty, backed up by self-respect, will easily make heroes of them. On this point, see what they did at Lucknow: remember the conduct of Sir Henry

Lawrence, their devout resignation, their calm and serious valour.

"What does the Indian officer do when he is not occupied in military duty? How does he kill time?" "Why, play games, of course," he says, with a flash of his blue eyes, in his quick, frank voice. "We play cricket, and hunt, and play polo. My regiment are famous polo-players. Our champions went out to America, and challenged the whole United States. The old Yankees couldn't touch them! We were proud, I can tell you." "Is the game rough?" "Oh yes!" he says; he himself has had his skull cracked, and a young officer of his regiment was killed at this game. Then they have football and tennis.

Three or four conversations with my hussar upon all the great topics—religion, morals, politics. He talks with admirable frankness, as Englishmen often do when you speak their language and they feel at their ease. He conversed with enthusiasm, with no effort to shine, and with no attempt to study my ideas inquisitively or critically. He had much to say, speaking with great sincerity, of what he considered "vital subjects." His ideas are very simple; he makes no attempt at philosophy. At once he speaks of God, the personal English divinity, with a mysticism singular in a creature so healthy and active. "Don't you know," he says, "it is only a matter of feeling, and it is impossible to prove that I am right, but I can't think that God doesn't take care of us. I am certain that God loves us. Just so a man can't prove that his wife loves him, and still he is sure she does. About the soul, I think it is a kind of double, inside the body. When a man dreams, his body is weighed down with sleep, but his soul lives, remains active, goes about. What do you suppose becomes of the human body, when it decays? Do you suppose it disappears entirely? No; this body contains a subtle essence, which may have the same form; and this essence lasts." These are the primitive notions of mankind, which, according to Herbert Spencer, mark the very earliest stage in the idea of a spiritual world. It is singular to meet them, so fervently expressed, in an English army officer. "Take the parable of the seed," he says. "The seed develops, becomes a plant; it is the same that it was at first; and still it is different. I think the soul develops like this, after death." He quotes Scripture, and speaks of Jesus Christ with affection and enthusiasm. "How can any one compare the Buddha with Christ?" he says. "What did Jesus gain by His teaching? Nothing but to be crucified."

To-night he put to me this question, which a Frenchman has to answer constantly in an English country: "Your novels give a very sad idea of France. Why are they so smutty? And how can we judge you, except from the descriptions your own people give, your Daudets and Zolas? It seems to me," he says, "that the proper work, the mission of the novelist, is to raise the level of morality, to be an educator. But yours are corrupters." I seek to explain to him the theory of the *roman expérimental*, the scientific method. "I don't understand this," he says. "What is the aim of science, if not to render mankind better and happier? Your people degrade it. Besides, if they *must* paint reality, why need they stir up all this mud? George Eliot, who is more realistic than the French, remains pure, all the same, and her novels give one strength. Life is not filthy; or, at least, such has not been my experience."

I believe it; his life is one of those successes in which the labour of a hundred generations results. An American writer has said that the English gentleman, developed in the open air, quietly established upon a few strong moral ideas, is one of the perfect specimens of our human nature, in his nobleness and in his happiness. This Englishman has behind him a wholesome and merry youth; he respects himself, he is a master of others; his beliefs are clearly defined, his activity and energy are overflowing. He married an innocent, merry little girl, a "child-wife," who reveres him as a hero, and with whom he is in love. He has scarcely seen anything that was not good and beautiful; the literature with which he is familiar is serious, moral, pure, and intentionally silent as to the dark lower levels of humanity. Certainly, he is not complex; he has not the quivering sensibility, the subtle perceptions of the heroes of our romances; but neither is he a saddened and nervous sceptic. His candour, his optimism, his freshness of nature, his happy and intact vitality, are those of a strong and virgin soul whose free development has been in no way checked or distorted.

The same is true of the three other officers on board, who are all going home on a year's leave. In the morning after their douche, attired in whimsical pajamas, they pace the dripping deck. Then, in short light coats and cloth caps and flannel trousers and canvas shoes, all day long they talk, they laugh, they eternally fill their short straight pipes with smooth English tobacco, they read inoffensive novels of simple morality and complicated plot. D. is the youngest, the most "boyish" of the four. But Captain M. is the most seriously, profoundly, and constantly cheerful. He also is a squire's son, and grew up in a corner of that patriarchal, bucolic England, now fast disappearing. "I liked the old farmers," he says; "they had a nice way, when they were in trouble, of coming to ask a bit of advice from my mother." In the morning, when he is dressing, we hear him singing like a blackbird in his cabin. He talks with everybody, and his radiant smile makes you happy to the bottom of your heart. At dinner, in evening dress, his big chest strains the broad starched surface of his shirt-front. Seated at the end of the table, where he carves huge "underdone" slices of roast beef, he is happier and grander than ever. To-day, January 1st, as he had beside him at table two young Italian girls, with whom he is carrying on the customary flirtation, he proposed : "Queen Margherita !" but in his everyday voice, and with a smile. Then he stood up ; and this time, his face all lighted up, looking slowly around him, solemnly he said : "Gentlemen, the Queen !" and I shall never forget the youthful enthusiasm with which the lieutenant of hussars rejoined : "God bless her !"

Miss M., of the Wesleyan missions, resides at Jaipur, where her duty is to visit the *zenanas* and make the acquaintance of the Hindu ladies as a friend, a missionary, and a teacher. Small, dry, flat, strong, with thin lips, with eye-glasses perched upon her aquiline nose, she walks the deck like a grenadier, in the company of one of the officers, or of Professor M., from the University of Bombay. At first sight, she is most unattractive. I think of those great, dark, timid eyes of the Indian women, of their silent grace and gentleness. One perceives them to be imaginative and impassioned, sensuous and dreamy. It is easy to understand how shocking to the Hindu must be the independence and the mannish ways of the Englishwoman.

She has described to me her life in Jaipur. She lives with another lady of the missions in a comfortable house furnished with punkahs, tatties,* and all English comforts. There is riding, with a groom in attendance, accompanied by dogs, and there is tennis-playing with the English residents. Here we have an English Sister of Charity, devoted,

---

* The tatty is a machine for producing a vapour of perfumed water in order to cool the room.

like our own, to a religious idea, toward which all the acts of her life converge, but preserving the exterior, the habits, the tone, of an Englishwoman of the middle class, the wife of an official or a doctor. Celibacy increases her freedom of action. She is not in any way secluded from the world. She surrounds herself with all the comforts of life. Her personality is not enfeebled under the action of a uniform rule; on the contrary, she has an individuality which would be remarkable in any woman. You feel her to be mistress of herself, and entirely secure; she respects herself, and is able to make herself respected by others. "I have never," she says, "been insulted by any Hindu; and yet I often go out alone on horseback. It is understood that I am a lady, and every one treats me as such."

She has had a Puritan education, without superior instruction and without broad intelligence. Narrow of mind, uncompromising, destitute of the sympathetic faculty—what does she know of the Hindu women to whom she has consecrated herself? What does she understand of the circumstances which have determined the condition of the wife and the widow in India? This religion which she labours with all her strength to destroy, "which we must eradicate from the country," she confuses with all the religious forms which are not her Protestant Christianity: "idolatry," the one word suffices to designate it. But the good woman is full of her subject: "We want to make these poor Hindu women happier, to get a little liberty for them, to teach them to think for themselves." That is to say, to make them European and English. She is always ready to talk about her "missionary work," her hopes, her methods. With what emotion she quotes the words: "Who is He, Lord, that I might believe on Him? I that speak unto thee am He." A text which, she says, produced a great impression upon a Musalman. The Hindu tolerance surprises her; it saddens her also, as proving their indifference. No husband has ever forbidden her visits to his wives. She is much beloved in the *zenanas*. "Come and see us," the Hindu ladies say to her, "we have need of you. Tell us about this Jesus, of whom the sahibs talk so much." They sing hymns: but, after all, these are only diversions from the monotony of imprisonment; they do not dream of becoming converted; all the moral and psychological conditions necessary for the establishment among them of a faith like Miss M.'s are entirely wanting. It would require generations, and a complete change of environment, to bring this about. One of them, to whom Miss M. had given two dolls, placed them at the foot of the Krishna, and bowed before them.

Miss M. talks religion to me; she lends me religious books; she demonstrates to me the "idolatry" of the Roman Catholic faith: she predicts to me the future extension and the supremacy of Wesleyan Protestantism; she speaks with pride of the usefulness and grandeur of her "work." The excellent, courageous woman! She is now on her way to

Scotland for a year's rest, after seven years of labour. Then she will return to resume the harness in Jaipur. When she becomes too old for service the missionary society will give her a comfortable pension. Meanwhile, alone, she leads a contented life; her existence is wholesome, industrious, and worthy of respect, resting upon a grand, serious idea. She aids in spreading civilisation, the civilisation of England. She labours for the ideal which her race has conceived. Life has a meaning for her. It is a combat with evil. When her last hour comes, she will fall peacefully asleep, "and God will gather His servant unto Him."

January 2.

It is a strange curiosity this, to interest one's self in the differences among the races of mankind, and their diverse fashions of looking at the world and regarding life, when one has the constant presence of this great monotonous sea, on which we have been borne forward for now eight days. After these conversations, perhaps as a result of them, one recurs easily to the Hindu thought, the Brahmanic dream.

At seven o'clock, after the bath, with bare feet in yellow grass slippers, you saunter upon the deck, now just washed down. A fresh, subtle air slips under the light clothing and enfolds you deliciously. You abandon yourself to the caress, and are happy in the happiness which all things diffuse. The spaces of sky and sea are full of a calm, broad radiance: the vast water is all penetrated with light, as with a great deep joy. Surely this water is not insensible; it rejoices or it is sad, as the sun broods upon it or deserts it. This universal motion, this vague, incessant sound, this light breath which stirs its surface, all declare it alive. It is a great divine being, for it is happy, very ancient, the simplest of things; for it is solitary, and its presence fills the world. Beyond the horizon, far in the south, spread boundless, following the curve of the globe, it shines the same, tranquil or astir, alone under the sky, unseen. No eye looks upon it; but it is there. What is it, then, in itself? Perchance a great elemental soul, limited to the world of feeling, scarcely capable of reverie, traversed by emotions very simple and very obscure, a delight in being alive, sadness, anger, depression, affection, desire, effort.

Close by the ship flame little green wavelets: a thousand little lives play on the surface of the great solitary being. They spring from it, are made of its substance. They rise, expand, quiver, run, whirl, sparkle, and are no more; and others rise in multitudes, in generations; and there is an incessant shiver of coming into existence, appearing and disappearing, without an instant's permanence, since at each imperceptible fraction of time, each little moving wavelet is composed of new water, so that, for the few moments of its life, nothing in it is permanent but its form. And yet, notwithstanding its nothingness, each is a distinct little individual, taking existence in its own way. There are idle ones, giddy ones, violent, rebellious, capricious ones. In front there is a bright sparkle of merry foam; along the ship's side a rapid running of murmuring water; behind it there are placid undulations of sinuous crystal, smooth surfaces as of great mirrors, which writhe slowly and noiselessly, where vague orange gleams shine, twist, and disappear; and beneath this moving diversity sleeps the dull water which has never risen to the surface, which knows not what it is to glitter in the sunlight. And yet, these mornings, even this is penetrated all through with light—an equal, motionless light, not disturbed by agitations of shadows like that of the quivering surface. And the whole ocean throws out a strong and gentle radiance which comes from its great inner spaces.

Overhead, the sky is very pale, whitish, with a lustre of molten opal. A peaceful troop of little clouds is moving across it very slowly. By degrees the space grows empty, the universal light traverses it, dwells in it, and fills it. Sometimes you feel passing over yourself, like a vague sadness, the shadow of the little mists that glide across the sun. No other event. Thought has put an end to itself; and so you forget that you are, and return into the quietude of that which is enduring, which never changes.

PORT SAID, *January* 7.

After the Hindu East, this Egyptian East is a very poor thing. Where are the bare bronzed skins of the swarming crowd under the Indian sun?

These people are too much clad, too much covered up, in their green petticoats.

Ugly, regular streets laid out at right angles, bordered with square shop-fronts covered with placards. An unpleasant odour rises from the brown sand underfoot. *Cafés-concerts*, shops of vile photographs, dry-goods establishments, succeed one another. A population of villainous Levantines. The place is a cosmopolitan hotel, where all ships set ashore their passengers; and it is abundantly supplied with all those pleasures which the sailor may desire after long voyages. There is nothing so sad and so unsightly as these hackneyed cross-roads which have no existence of their own, and only live by the continuous passage of strangers in search of amusement. There is nothing here but a little European scum flung down upon the edge of the desert, in which all the streets come to an end so strangely.

At the very extremity of the town, in the Arab quarter, we go to see some dancing-girls from Upper Egypt. Tobacco smoke, torn into bluish clouds, envelops in a low, close hall a curious crowd of various nationalities: Arabs, negroes, Europeans, Copts. An Abyssinian woman, a kind of Hottentot Venus, whose stout brown figure shows through the transparency of her white garment, advances on tiptoe, with a negro smile, following the incomprehensible rhythm of the music. Suddenly she stops, entirely motionless. Then a horrible thing, indescribable: slowly her back begins to shiver under her white garment, trembles, is agitated by successive shocks, vibrates strangely; then, with writhings of the hips, sinking to the ground, half-rising, she sways to and fro, like some creeping beast that has been wounded and is about to die.

Then appears upon the scene, with unnoticed entrance, a very young Arab girl. A strange, cold smile upon her haughty lips, her eyes half closed, slowly and disdainfully throwing back her head, her slender young figure rigid, the chest advanced, she stretches out both arms, all the fingers quivering. Meanwhile, noiselessly, with a rapidity of sinuous motion that is like a snake, a third spins around the hall, describing complicated circles. Closely draped in red velvet, her black hair drawn tightly around her flat head, her outlines angular and precise, the body very long, impassive, with sphinx-like smile, she has the figure, the aspect, the features of the old Egyptian drawings. Throwing herself to the left with an abrupt jerk of the hips, throwing herself to the right, monotonously she glides in circles with ever-increasing rapidity—a sombre being whose silence and gravity are enigmatical; sometimes stopping suddenly, while something like a slow spasm runs over her whole figure, then moving forward, in a kind of magic circle, around the two *almehs*. At last, in the stupor which the monotony of Oriental music causes, you cease to distinguish the three dancing figures; you only see the endless intricacy of lines, which they describe, yourself hypnotised, as at sight of a long-continued juggling with glittering balls.

Next door, a *café chantant*. Seated in rows upon cushions, cross-legged, the musicians are scraping on their strings, swaying backward and forward to the rhythm. One of them I notice: he has the strange, gentle, sleepy eyes of the dreamer, and a faint, unchanging smile. I feel that he could sit there all night, smiling always, and drawing from his cithar the same eternal Oriental phrase.

Upon a platform three women are seated. In the centre, a fat and slatternly Syrian, with banged hair. At the right, a Copt, in a shabby dark garment, loaded with brass necklaces, feeble-looking and depressed, in an attitude of inexpressible fatigue and sadness. At the left, a very young Arab girl, slender, wrapped tightly in her white drapery, extremely erect, her long-fringed eyelids cast down, an air at once imperious and savage. At certain cadences in the chant which the cithars are repeating, her voice is heard, her whole figure grows more erect still, it stiffens, and there is an almost imperceptible shiver from head to foot; the thin nostrils dilate, and even the finger-tips vibrate. In this frail form, as in the chant, there is harshness, there is sensuousness, and, most of all, unutterable pride. And an hour long this music trembles, complicated and childish, without recognisable *motif*, made of subtle discords, quarter-tones, that could not be written out. After twenty minutes of it, you feel its strange, sad, sensuous charm. It is absorbing and monotonous, like those Saracenic designs and mosaics in whose complex and infinite interlacing you lose yourself; like those dances of *almehs* whose slow entanglements and undulations the Orientals can follow through a whole night. It is like the intoxication of opium or of hashish; and one could stay for hours, spell-bound by the succession of chants and the slender music, following, as in a confused dream, the sudden growing erect and shivering of the Arab figure.

There is no spectacle, no book, no study, which brings you so abruptly and so far into the soul of a stranger race as do ten notes of its music. Nothing gives so fully the sensation of the distance which separates us from them. A Musalman chant, heard suddenly in the evening, as you pass by a mosque; a Buddhist chime, flinging out its call in the abrupt twilight, in the depths of an amazing Cinhalese forest, where the serried trunks of the cocoanut-palms mirror themselves in the red water of stagnant ponds; Hindu gongs, heathen trumpets, vibrating upon the high terraces of Benares, as the sun is sinking beyond the roseate Ganges: all these are sudden openings, they are abrupt flashes, which for an instant throw a strong light and reveal everything. In recollections of these are summed up, are fused, all the sensations of a journey. And here one feels the Arab life, the encampments and the marches of ancestors in the silence and monotony of the desert, and the Semitic soul, dominant, traversed by sudden shocks and by impulses of violent will.

January 11.

Yesterday evening, about ten o'clock, we came into bad weather. All night long, tossing in my berth, I hear the uproar of the black water outside, and of objects pitching about within. At last it benumbs and stupefies one, this tumult which enters one's dreams; and with eyes open, in an odd condition of somnolence, one submits, like an inert thing, to the action of the tremendous power which is at work in the darkness.

At daylight the air has grown cold and we shiver. We are off Crete. A sea tumultuous and livid like the sky; ragged clouds hanging low, waves rising from the deep, mingle, rush, fly, in a grey fog, a salt vapour, with a clamour of wind and water. And all day long the ship falls, falls into black valleys; rises staggering under a mass of blue-green dripping foam; gets above the horizon, which has lost its level, above the great circle of pallid sea, which oscillates upon the wan sky as if shaken in its very depths.

In the evening there is a little peace overhead, but the heavy seas are running as madly as ever. In the distance crests of waves shine, like whitish lightning, upon the grey tumult of the water.

A northern twilight, interminable and cold; a red bar, a gleam fixed in the horizon, which lingers there sadly for hours, which seems as if it would never disappear, and toward which we advance steadily. A sad return into sombre Europe!

INDEX

INDEX

A

ADEN, 4-6
Agra, Mogul capital, 165; tomb of Akbar, 165, 166; citadel, 167-72; Taj, 172-77
Akbar, Mogul emperor, Musalman, 165; his tomb, 165, 166; his palace, 168-72
Allahabad, its worship of snakes, 94
Almehs, Egyptian, at Port Said, 262-65
Amiel, a Hindu mind, 137-40
Animals, Hindu worship of, 93, 94, 96, 105, 106, 145, 156, 176
Arab dancing-girls, 263-65
Architecture, Cinhalese, 21; Hindu, 78, 147, 148, 187-89, 208, 235-38; Musalman, 82, 158, 166-76, 191
Aurungzebe, 181
Autonomy of India, possible, 17, 67, 100, 160, 161

B

BABUS (native merchants), 56, 96, 108, 109, 200, 219
Bayaderes, at Pondichéry, 48
Benares, sacred city of Brahmanism, 74-76; first impressions of, 76; scenes by the river in the morning, 78-82, 140-42; palace of the Maharajah, 105; temple of the monkeys, 106; the University, 106; shop, 109; dancing-girls, 110-14; street scenes, 142-45; temple of Siva, 145-48; last look at, 156, 157.
Bengalis, appearance and character of, 53-55

Bindrabun, sacred city, abounding in monkeys, 186 ; temples in honour of Krishna, 187
Bo, the sacred tree of Ceylon, 22
Bombay, cosmopolitan city, 219-23 ; atmospheric effects, 222, 223, 229; street scenes, 223-26 ; hospital for animals, 226 ; English placards, 226 ; Salvation Army, 227-29 ; Parsi worship, 229 ; Parsi cemetery, 230-32 ; point of departure for Europe, 248
Brahmá and Bráhmă, 120, 128-32, 242
Brahmanism, its ceremonials, 79-92 ; theology, 92-97, 148-55 ; ethics, 94-100 ; vision of the world and of life, 116-31, 146-48
Brahmans, highest caste of Hindus, 74-76, 84-93, 116
Brahmo-Somaj, new sect of "Young Bengal," 154, 214
Buddha (Gautama), Sakya-Muni, statues of, in Ceylon, 22, 31 ; a Brahman of Benares, 75 ; his statues in cave temples of Elura, 244-47
Buddhism in Ceylon, its ceremonial, monasteries, characteristic features, 21-26, 30-38 ; in India, its date unknown, 140 ; absorbed by Hinduism, 154 ; perpetuated in the caves of Elura, 244

C

CALCUTTA, arrival at, 52 ; first impressions of, 52-54
Caste system of India, 91
Cemetery, English, at Lucknow, 159 ; Parsi, at Bombay, 230-32
Ceylon, approach to, 11 ; first impressions, 12-16 ; aspect of the country, 12, 15, 16, 18-21
Cheddy Lal, the Sudra "boy," 161-64, 192 ; his opinions of the English, 163, 164, 216 ; of the Salvation Army and the missionaries, 229
Chunder Dutt, converted babu, 201
Cinhalese, their appearance and character, 12, 15-18, 28

INDEX 271

D

DARJILING, arrival at, 63; English character of the place, 63-68, 73
Delhi, a great capital, its fortress, 190, 191; its mosque, 191; its shawl merchants, 192-94
Dupleix, statue of, at Pondichéry, 49
Durga, a Hindu divinity, 81, 92, 93

E

ELEPHANTS, 20, 28, 204, 206-208
Elura, cave temples of, 233-47
English authors studied in India, 100, 101, 108, 213, 214; English conviction of duty toward India, 66-68, 160, 201, 257; English influence, effects of, in Ceylon, 17, 18; and in India, 67, 200, 202; English judges in India, their impartiality, 163; English life and manners transplanted into India, 52, 53, 63-68; English officers, met on shipboard, 249-56; English soldiers in India, 66, 164, 198; Englishwoman, a missionary, met on shipboard, 256-59

G

GANESA, Hindu divinity, 77, 81, 90, 93, 143, 208, 219
Ganges, the river, below Calcutta (the Hugli), 50-52, 78-81; at Benares, 140-42, 156, 157; an object of worship, 84, 89; "the divine Mother," 90; an image of Hinduism, 155

H

HIMALAYAS, the, first sight of, 58; backbone of the earth, 59; forests of, 60; mixed population of the foot-hills, 60-62; change of temperature on approaching, 61; seen from Darjiling, 62, 63, 68, 69, 72, 73

Hinduism, a development of Brahmanism, 148 ; its complicated character, 148-55

Hindus, their peculiar ethics, 94-99 ; their souls a mystery to us, 99-103 ; their relations to the European races, 103 ; the nautch their greatest pleasure, 113, 114; peculiarities of their mental organisation, 139, 148

I

INDRA, Vedic divinity, his statues in cave temples of Elura, 234
Instruction in India, 99, 100, 106, 107, 212-15

J

JAHAN, Shah, builder of the Taj, 172
Jains, Hindu Buddhists, their sanctuaries in the caves of Elura, 235, 244
Jaipur, capital of Rajputana, 203 ; street scenes, 204-208 ; buildings, 208 ; tiger cage, 210 ; temple of Siva, 211 ; college, 212-15 ; scenic effect, 215
Jews, at Aden, 4
Jumna, the river, "the divine Mother," 90 ; at Agra, 167 ; scenes on its banks, 184-86

K

KAILASA, the Himalayan paradise of Siva, 76, 97 ; the great temple of the caves of Elura, 235-38
Kali, Hindu goddess, 77, 92, 98, 99, 214
Kandy, ancient capital of Ceylon, 21-31
Kasi, name for Benares, 75, 76
Kelanya Ganga, river of Ceylon, 19
Krishna, incarnation of Vishnu, 152 ; specially worshipped at Muttra, 180 ; "the blue god," divinity of the pre-Aryan

INDEX 273

inhabitants of India, 181; story of his life, 181-84; poem concerning him, 183; his temple at Bindrabun, 186, 187, 203
Kshatriyas, warrior caste of Hindus, 105, 130, 204, 208, 219
Kunchain-Junga, a peak of the Himalayas, 62, 63; seen at sunrise, 68, 69
Kutab-Minar, tower near Delhi, 194-96

L

LAMA'S temple near Darjiling, 66, 71, 72
Lawrence, General Henry, tomb of, at Cawnpur, 159
Lucknow, a Mohammedan and English city, 158; siege of, 159, 251

M

MADHAVA, Hindu author (fourteenth century), 152
Malabar Hill, 230-32
Maya, the goddess, 129, 134, 202
Meditations, the five Buddhist, 24, 25
Missionary, Wesleyan, to Jaipur, 256-59
Monastery, Buddhist, in Kandy, 21-26
Mongol types in Northern India, 58, 61
Monkeys, 106, 197
Monks, Buddhist, their rules of life, 23-26
Mosques in Benares, 82; in Lucknow, 158; in Delhi, 191, 195
Mumtaz-i-Mahal, her tomb, the Taj, 172
Music, Oriental, its strange character, 264

N

NANA SAHIB, 114
Nautch, the, 111-14
Negroes, at Aden, 4, 5

S

P

PANTHEISM, Hindu, 124-32
Parsis in Bombay, 221, 222, 230
Parvati, Hindu goddess, wife of Siva, 92, 212, 239
Peacocks, blue, 195, 197, 216, 217
Peradinya Gardens, 40, 41
Perusha, 94
Pictures, two Hindu, 116-24
Pondichéry, arrival at, 44 ; French element in, 44-46, 49 ; aspect of, 46 ; statue of Dupleix in, 49

R

RAILWAYS in Ceylon, 18 ; in India, 56, 161-65, 200, 219, 220, 233
Rainfall of Northern India, 59
Rajputs, very ancient Aryan people, 203
Rama, incarnation of Vishnu, 97, 152
Rig-Veda, 86

S

SAKTISTS, a Hindu sect, 98, 99
Sakya-Muni (Gautama), *see* Buddha
Salvation Army in India, 227-29
Samunda, Hindu goddess, 92
Sanskrit, 100, 107, 213
Scots Greys, in India, 158, 198
Sepoys, 96, 106, 221
Shawl merchants of Delhi, 192-94
Shelley, a Hindu mind, 135-37
Shipboard, life on, 1-10, 44, 49-52, 248-51, 258
Sikkim, the, 64, 69, 73
Siliguri, 58

INDEX   275

Siva, Hindu god, 81, 90, 92, 93, 96-99, 105, 130, 143, 146, 150, 151, 225, 226, 234-47
Soldiers, English, at Aden, 4; in India, 66, 158, 164, 167, 198
Sudra, low caste of Hindus, 78, 91, 104, 163, 219
Surya, Hindu god, 90, 126, 234

T

TAJ, the, tomb of Mumtaz-i-Mahal, 172-77
Tavernier, French traveller in India (1641), 181
Tea-planters in Ceylon, 42
Temples: Buddhist, in Kandy, 21, 22, 31, 32, 38; Hindu, at Villianur, 47-49; Lama's, at Darjiling, 70, 71; in Benares, 80, 105, 144-46; at Muttra, 181; in Bindrabun, 186, 187; in Jaipur, 211; in caves of Elura, 234-39, 244-47
Tigers, caged, in Jaipur, 210
Trichinopoli, pagodas of, 48, 181

U

UPANISHADS, the, 86, 107; extracts from, 117-24; meaning of the word, 120, *note;* singular character of, 139; contain much modern thought, 214

V

VEDAS, the, 125, 126, 129, 130
Vegetation, tropical, of Ceylon, 11, 12, 15, 16, 18-21, 26-30, 39-42; of India, 50, 60, 69, 220
Villages, their organisation in India, 178; picturesque aspect, 178
Villianur, pagoda of, 47-49
Vishnu, Hindu god, 85, 86-90, 93, 97, 130, 149-53, 180, 225, 234

W

WALES, the Prince of, in Ceylon, 26; his portrait in Benares, 105

Z

ZENANAS, 112, 256, 258
Zend-Avesta, quoted, 231

THE END

Printed by BALLANTYNE, HANSON & CO.
Edinburgh and London

www.ingramcontent.com/pod-product-compliance
Lightning Source LLC
Chambersburg PA
CBHW031250250426
43672CB00029BA/1917